THE SUCCESSFUL LIS PROFESSIONAL

MANAGING YOUR ORGANIZATION

Elizabeth Parker

LIBRARY ASSOCIATION PUBLISHING
LONDON

Published by
Library Association Publishing
7 Ridgmount Street
London WC1E 7AE

Library Association Publishing is wholly owned by The Library Association.

First published 1999

British Library Cataloguing in Publication Data
A catalogue record for this book is available from the British Library.

ISBN 1-85604-335-5

Typeset in 11/14pt Aldine 721 by Library Association Publishing
Printed and made in Great Britain by MPG Books Ltd, Bodmin, Cornwall.

Contents

Series Editor's preface

With rapid technological advances and new freedoms, the workplace presents a dynamic and challenging environment. It is just these advances, however, that necessitate a versatile and adaptable workforce which appreciates that lifelong full-time jobs are a thing of the past. Work is being contracted out, de-structured organizations are emerging, and different skills and approaches are required from all workers who must solve new and changing problems. These workers must become self motivated, multi-skilled and constantly learn. Demonstrating the international economic importance of professional development, the European Commission has officially voiced its support for a European community committed to lifelong learning.

For the information professional, the key to success in this potentially destabilizing context is to develop the new skills the workplace demands. Above all, the LIS professional must actively prioritize a commitment to continuous professional development. The information industry is growing fast and the LIS profession is experiencing very rapid change. This series has been designed to help you manage change by ensuring the growth of your own portfolio of professional skills. By reading these books you will have begun the process of seeing yourself as your own best resource and accepting the rewarding challenge of staying ahead of the game.

The series is very practical, focusing on specific topics relevant to all types of library and information service. Recognizing that your time is precious, these books have been written so that they may be easily read and digested. They include instantly applicable ideas and techniques which you can put to the test in your own workplace, helping you to succeed in your job.

The authors have been selected because of their practical experience and enthusiasm for their chosen topic and we hope you will benefit from their advice and guidance. The points for reflection, checklists and summaries are designed to provide stepping stones for you to assess your understanding of the topic as you read.

Records are a vital business and information resource, and by definition they relate specifically to an organization's own business and may be unique and irreplaceable. The increasing availability and sophistication of information technology means that more records are produced now than ever before, and in a greater variety of formats. As the only directly employed 'information person' in your organization, you, as the library and information service professional may find yourself, whether you like it or not, responsible for the organization's records. Don't worry if this is the case, because in *Managing your organization's records*, Elizabeth Parker introduces LIS professionals at all levels to records management. The book takes you step by step through the necessary procedures and shows you how to manage an organization's records efficiently, effectively and economically.

It will also serve as a deskbook when help is needed with specific types of records, and addresses many questions, such as:

> ➤ is it a record or not?
> ➤ where to store active records
> ➤ storage, preservation and retrieval of records
> ➤ what to do in the case of a disaster
> ➤ ways and means to get your message across the organization to convince the staff that records are serious business.

Elizabeth Parker's experience as a records manager, trainer and consultant gives her a unique opportunity to help all LIS Professionals whichever background area they are working in.

Books in this series are intentionally short in length and are intended to help the busy professional, therefore they cannot deal with all these situations in great detail, but the case studies play a valuable role in illustrating ideas and in addition the lists of other information sources will allow the reader to follow up on any point.

I am sure you will benefit from reading this book and putting the ideas into action. May I wish you enjoyment and satisfaction in your endeavours to manage the records of your organization successfully!

Sheila Pantry, OBE

Acknowledgments

I would like to thank all the friends and colleagues who encouraged me to write this book and supported me through the process. In particular Sheila, for her patient guidance, and Helen and Beth at the LA for helping me to understand 'how books work'. Above all Peter Emmerson in both of his roles – husband delivering tea and sympathy (Aren't you finished yet?'), and colleague providing invaluable advice and support. My children ('Keep going, Mummy! You can do it.') also deserve a special 'thank you' – they had to go out without me too often.

Introduction

Organizations run on records. They are a vital and unique source of

> *information* for the management and development of an organization and its business
> *evidence* of the organization's activities and conduct
> *knowledge* about its expertise, work and achievements.

In short, records are a mission-critical business resource. And like all other resources – buildings, equipment, cash and people – they need to be managed if they are to add value to the business, to be an asset rather than a liability. But if you're a librarian and you've been given responsibility for managing your organization's records, you may well feel that you've drawn the short straw. 'Why me?', you say, 'What do I know about records?' Even if you're enthusiastic about the idea of taking on something new, your next thought is likely to be along the lines of 'Where do I start?'

Well, start here. This is a book about records management for librarians and other information professionals who have responsibilities for records, but no formal training in records management. It will give you an overview of what 'managing records' means, the key issues and best practice. Whether you need to provide records management services, develop a records retention policy or help people to set up filing systems, it will help you to plan what to do and how to approach it. It will also help you to recognize your limitations and to recognize where you really need help or advice from a professional records manager.

I use six organizations as examples throughout the book. These are:

> an architectural practice
> a pharmaceutical company
> a management consultancy firm
> a charity
> a local authority
> a university.

Whatever your organization's business is, you should be able to relate to one of these. By the way, I use the term 'business' with a small 'b', meaning 'the work of the organization'. If you don't work in a multinational corporation, this book is still for you.

There's one important issue to clear up before we go any further. You can't be solely responsible for managing your organization's records. Whatever your job description says, you as an individual can't be given and can't take sole responsibility for managing your organization's records. As with any other business resource, the organization's legal officers are ultimately responsible and accountable for ensuring that the organization's records are properly managed. Depending on what type of organization it is, this may mean the Board of Directors, the Managing Partners or the Senate. In practical terms they delegate this responsibility to every employee. So managing the organization's records is *everybody's* responsibility. Of course, in order to fulfil their responsibilities, staff have to know what to do and how to do it. Policies and procedures need to be developed, and everyone has to be trained to use them. Which may be where you come in. But you can't do this alone either. To develop policies and procedures, you will need input from other specialists such as lawyers, auditors and compliance officers, and from the managers who run the business and the staff who generate the records. We'll deal with how you approach this later. For now, just remember that you're not in this alone.

Part 1
Records and records management

Introduction

Before you can manage records, you need to know what records are, and what managing them means. In particular, you need to understand what makes records records, and how they are different from other types of materials which you are used to managing in a library or information centre.

Chapter 1
What are records?
And why manage them?

In this chapter you'll find out:

➤ **what records are**
➤ **why it's important to manage records**
➤ **what records management is**
➤ **the benefits of managing records, and the risks of not doing so.**

What are records?

Records are *documents or other items* containing recorded information, which are produced or received *as part of a business activity*.

Documents or other items

We are all familiar with documents. Most of us handle too many of them every day. Let's try the word association test. If I say 'document', what do you say? If you said 'paper', you're not alone. Most of us have some preconceptions about what is and isn't a document, based on our own experiences. There are plenty of hair-splitting academic definitions of a 'document', but let's keep it simple here. What you need to remember is:

1 A document can be in any medium and any format:
   - paper: any size, any type
   - film: any size and format, including microfilm
   - magnetic: computer disks and tapes
   - optical: WORM disk, CD-ROM, CD-R

2 A document can contain *any* kind of data or information:

Paper documents can contain text, graphics and images. They can even have things attached to them, like birthday cards with squeakers on the front. Electronic documents can also contain text, graphics and images, plus whizzy things like sound and video clips. Have you sent anyone an Internet birthday card yet? It's a document. So are all of these:

- an A0 size print of a floor plan *and* the electronic version of the plan held in the CAD (Computer Aided Design) system
- an electronic version of a Powerpoint slide presentation with embedded video clips and graphics *and* the hard copy handouts
- a paper copy of a technical report *and* an electronic copy and a microfilm copy
- a letter on letterhead paper *and* the electronic version on the hard drive of the PC
- an electronic mail message *and* the printed version for your paper files!
- a Post-it™ note with a scribbled message or comment
- a diary with some entries
- a supplier's catalogue
- a photographic print.

So what about other items ? Well, anything, literally anything, can be a record, either because it can be interpreted to provide information, or because it illustrates or substantiates information in other forms. You are probably familiar with video and audio tapes, x-rays and digital recordings such as those made by tachometers in lorries and 'black boxes' on aircraft. Here are some things which you might not immediately think of as records, but the people who produce and use them certainly do:

- samples of chemical compounds generated by research in a pharmaceutical company
- samples of rock collected during geological surveys by an oil exploration company
- samples of seeds retained by an agricultural company

> test pieces of steel retained by a quality control unit in a steelmaking plant
> body fluid and tissue samples analysed in a pathology laboratory.

Among the weird and wonderful things I've come across in fifteen years are a three-foot-long section of a railway sleeper (a vital piece of evidence 'attached' to court records), an envelope containing 50-year-old cannabis leaves and seeds (in a police investigation file), a lock of hair (don't ask!) and one shoe (the other one is presumably lying on a road somewhere). Perhaps the best recent example to illustrate the range of things which can be records is the evidence collected by the Office of the Independent Counsel in the course of its investigation of the Clinton–Lewinsky affair in the United States. The investigation records included paper documents, computer files including e-mail messages, answering-machine tapes, a dress belonging to Ms Lewinsky and gifts given to her by the President.

So don't worry about the physical form of anything. If it looks like a record and feels like a record, it probably is a record. Even if it doesn't look or feel like a record, it might still be a record.

Some types of records are common to all organizations and all kinds of work – things like letters, reports, minutes of meetings and project files. Some records appear in most organizations in some form or another because the activities which generate them are common. For example:

> most organizations recruit staff, and recruitment activities generate records such as job application forms, interview notes and employment contracts
> most organizations buy things, and purchasing activities generate records such as purchase requisitions, purchase orders, delivery notes and invoices.

Other records are unique to particular types of organization, or industry sector, or type of work. These are the records which are generated by an organization's *real* business – manufacturing light bulbs, selling cars, staging tennis tournaments or whatever. To illustrate this, here are some of the records generated by three of our six organizations.

Architectural practice, project teams
Project files containing:

➤ correspondence with the client regarding design issues
➤ notes of design meetings with the client and contractors
➤ design specifications
➤ drawings and sketches
➤ design boards
➤ models
➤ samples of materials: bricks, glass, tiles, carpets, paints, fabrics.

Pharmaceutical company, drug development division
Clinical Trial Master Files containing:

➤ trial protocols
➤ samples of drug packaging and labelling
➤ patient records
➤ adverse reaction reports
➤ raw data from analytical instruments
➤ analytical reports
➤ study reports.

Local authority, trading standards department
Prosecutions files containing:

➤ correspondence, notes of meetings and reports relating to the prosecution
➤ legal briefs
➤ samples or examples of the items which were the subject of the prosecution: anything from food containers to toys, items of clothing or computer software.

Exercise

Without moving from where you are now, without looking at anything or asking anyone, make a list of the key records which your organization generates in the course of conducting its core business. Ask a colleague, ideally in another department, to do the same. Now compare your lists. Are you surprised by how much or how little you know? Well, at least now you know what you know. We'll come back to what you need to know in Chapter 11.

Part of a business activity

A record is something which is generated by a business (small b!) activity, as part of a business process, and its existence is evidence of the fact that the activity and process took place. This 'evidential' quality is one of the things which distinguishes records from other types of information resources. You can also look at it the other way round. Records are not things which are produced or received and retained solely for reference purposes. Let's look at a couple of examples to make this clearer.

Charity

The office manager regularly receives catalogues from companies which supply office equipment. He never looks at these when they arrive in the mail. His secretary files them in a series of boxes according to the type of equipment: chairs, photocopiers and so on. These catalogues are not records – they are received and kept purely for reference purposes.

When the office manager decides to buy new photocopiers, he gets out the 'Photocopiers' box and looks through the catalogues. He calls a few companies to get the latest prices. He decides which machine to buy and raises a purchase order which he sends to the supplier. He asks his secretary to set up a new capital purchase file. She sets up the file and puts in the catalogue which contains the details of the photocopiers which have been ordered (or maybe just the relevant page if

(cont.)

Charity (continued)

it's a large catalogue), the second copy of the purchase order and a copy of the covering letter to the supplier. The catalogue in the capital purchase file has become a record because it was used for a specific purpose as part of the purchasing activity.

Pharmaceutical company, drug development division
The scientists undertake research projects. They generate many types of records in the course of their analytical work in the laboratories. These are filed in research project files which are maintained by technicians and secretaries. The scientists document the final results of their work in the form of technical reports which typically contain text, graphs and charts, copies of printouts from analytical instruments and photographic prints.

When a report is completed, two copies are filed in the relevant research project file. These are obviously records. One copy is sent to the research library where a full set of technical reports is kept as a reference resource for other staff. This set is a reference collection – not a record.

Why do records need to be managed?

It's important to manage records because

> ➤ they are an organization's most important information resource
> ➤ they provide evidence of an organization's activities and conduct
> ➤ they are expensive to produce and keep.

Records are an organization's most important information resource

In a 1996 British Library study, managers in various business sectors were asked about their use of different sources of information, and their perceptions of the relative value of each source. They said that internal sources were used and valued more than external sources. The most popular and valued internal resources included 'personal files' and 'internal memos and reports'. This was no surprise to records managers. An organization's records are a unique and largely irreplaceable source of information about its work and achievements. They contain its accumulated experience, expertise and knowledge:

> ➤ what it has done, where, when and how
> ➤ why it did it in a particular way
> ➤ who was involved in it
> ➤ who was affected by it
> ➤ what resulted from it.

Organizations need records, and the information they contain, to operate day to day:

> ➤ to plan – most planning is done on the basis of previous experience
> ➤ to control – management need to be informed about the state of the business
> ➤ to make decisions – decisions are made at all levels of every organization every day, and most people feel more comfortable about making decisions when they have relevant information to hand
> ➤ to communicate – with their customers and suppliers, shareholders and staff, regulators and the public
> ➤ to protect their interests – paying what they owe and claiming what's due to them, protecting their property and reputations.

They need them to learn from the past, to support their current work and to plan for the future. If you're in any doubt about the value of records as an information resource, talk to an organization which has lost its records in a fire or other disaster (see Chapter 4).

Records provide evidence of an organization's activities and conduct

Because records are integral parts of the business activities and processes which generate them, they provide evidence of those activities and processes. They also provide evidence of an organization's:

> ➤ competence and integrity
> ➤ compliance with the law, and with regulations and standards relevant to its business
> ➤ concerns for business ethics and the interests of its stakeholders: employees and shareholders, customers and suppliers, pensioners, local communities and the general public.

Or the opposite, as the case may be! There have been plenty of cases reported in the press in the last ten years to demonstrate the power of records as evidence. Sometimes these cases reflected well on the organizations concerned, sometimes not. Have a look at the Turner & Newall example in Appendix 2.

Records are expensive to produce and keep

ALL records are expensive to maintain and store. Yes, even electronic records, because it's not just about the cost of storage – you have to look at the big picture. But let's start with storage. Records need to be put somewhere. And that means:

1 Space – ALL space costs money. It's as simple as that.
2 Equipment and supplies – these cost money too. No matter how hard you try, there just aren't that many free samples.
3 People – records don't file, store and retrieve themselves. People do it, and people are expensive.

Now you're convinced that records need to be managed, you need to know about records management.

What is records management?

Records management is *systematic* and *consistent control* of *all records throughout their lifecycle.*

Systematic

Records need to be managed in a planned and methodical way, by design rather than by accident.

Consistent

Records need to be managed consistently. There are two elements to this:

1 *Consistency of approach*. Records of the same kind should be managed in the same way. A simple example is correspondence. Correspondence about something important is important. It doesn't matter whether it's in the form of a typed letter on headed notepaper, a handwritten sheet from an A4 pad or an e-mail message. On the other hand, correspondence about something unimportant is unimportant, however fancy the paper or the computer.

2 *Consistency over time*. If managing records is worth doing, it's always worth doing. Not just in the good times when share prices are up and budgets flow freely and management are at peace with the world, but in the bad times too, when resources are scarce and executives are losing sleep over their results. Records need consistent attention and resources.

Control

Everything that happens to records needs to be controlled: how they are produced or received, organized and indexed, stored and retrieved, retained, and destroyed or stored permanently as archives.

All records

This includes documents and all the other weird and wonderful things which can be records. Active ones and inactive ones. Formal ones and informal ones. All of them.

Throughout their lifecycle

Records have a more complex lifecycle than other kinds of information resources. Figure 1.1 illustrates the stages in the records' lifecycle.

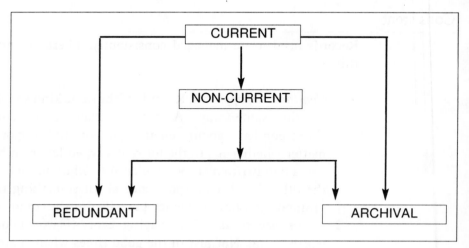

Fig. 1.1 *The stages in the records' lifecycle*

> ➤ CURRENT records are records which are needed to conduct current business
> ➤ NON-CURRENT records are records which are not needed to support current business, but which need to be retained for operational, legal or regulatory reasons
> ➤ ARCHIVAL records are records which are retained permanently because of their value for reference and research purposes
> ➤ REDUNDANT records are records which are no longer required, and which are not archival.

This lifecycle is based on value and use, not on time. Most records progress logically through the lifecycle, from current to non-current to archives or destruction. But some records will never be non-current. When they are no longer current, they will have no other value and will be destroyed immediately. Alternatively, it will be obvious when some records are created that they should be kept permanently, and they will become archival as soon as they are no longer current. However, records can move backwards as well as forwards through the lifecycle. Non-current records and archival records can become current again, and redundant records on the point of destruction can be rescued to be used another day. Here's a fairly common example.

The life of a record

A. Swindler was a sales manager with a company which manufactured office equipment. In May 1991 he submitted an expense claim for a business trip to Hong Kong. The claim was processed and paid by the accounts department, and the form was filed (current). It was kept in the office until the end of the financial year when the year's expense claims were transferred to storage, to be retained for six years for VAT purposes (non-current). Over the years Swindler submitted one too many big expense claims. The internal audit department suspected fraud and began an investigation in March 1998. They retrieved every box of expense claims from storage. These dated back to 1991. They removed all of Swindler's claims and put them into their investigation file (current again). Swindler was duly prosecuted and dismissed. The investigation file was transferred to storage for six years for legal reasons (non-current again) and was then destroyed (redundant).

Even some 'destroyed' records can be resurrected and become current again. Data recovery – finding and restoring data 'deleted' from magnetic media – is a booming business.

The lifecycle of a record can last one week, three months, 100 years – or indefinitely if the record is archival. Current records might have been created yesterday or twenty years ago. Whether records go forwards or backwards through the lifecycle, and however long this takes, doesn't matter. What does matter is that they are positively managed from birth to death, from the in-tray, keyboard or printer to the dustbin, shredder or incinerator.

So records management isn't – or isn't just – about 'filing' or 'archiving' or 'scanning', although these may all be part of it. And it's certainly not – or at least not just – about saving space or money.

What are the benefits of managing records?

There are four key benefits of managing records effectively: reliable information resources, complete evidence of business activities and processes, minimum costs and an improved working environment.

Reliable information resources

Complete and accurate records in the right place at the right time for everyone to do their work leads to efficiency and effectiveness all round. No confusion over different versions of the same document means no embarrassment in front of customers or shareholders. No records lost or unintentionally destroyed means no need to reinvent the wheel.

Complete evidence

No gaps in the record ensures more straightforward audits and reduced legal risks.

Minimum costs

No space, equipment or stationery wasted storing unnecessary records. No time wasted looking for records instead of using them.

Improved working environment

No piles on the floor means fewer things to trip over. No piles on top of cabinets means nothing to fall on top of people. No piles anywhere means a much more pleasant working environment and less stress for everybody.

You can also look at it the other way round. The risks of *not* managing records are: unreliable information (or none at all!), gaps in the record (or too many records!), uncontrolled costs, clutter and security risks.

Unreliable information – or none at all

On average, up to 10% of staff time is spent looking for records and information. What does this cost?

> **The cost of looking for information**
> The average working week is 37.5 hours. 10% of 37.5 hours is 45 minutes a day. The average salary is £20,000. So,
>
> ➢ for an organization with 50 employees, that's £100,000 a year
> ➢ for an organization with 500 people, that's £1 million a year
> ➢ for an organization with 5000 employees, that's £10 million a year.
>
> Every year, and rising all the time. And this is only the salary costs. You need to add 20–30% to calculate the fully built-up employment costs, depending on the type of organization.

Gaps in the record – or too many records

Records which are lost or inadvertently destroyed can create what auditors and lawyers call 'gaps in the record'. What you may see as 'just a few missing documents – no problem' could be interpreted as 'concealing evidence' or 'destroying incriminating documents', with very serious consequences. On the other hand, records which are not needed but are kept, through inefficiency or carelessness, can seriously damage an organization's interests – see Appendix 2 where it's likely that many of the documents which were finally disclosed to the lawyers in this example could and should have been destroyed years before. If they had been destroyed, there may have been less incriminating evidence against the company, which would obviously have been to its advantage. I'm not arguing a moral case here, only one for effective records management.

Uncontrolled costs

The more uncontrolled records are, the more . . .

. . . people keep
everything because

they keep everything
and they can't find
anything because

they're scared to
throw anything
away because

they don't know
what they've got
because

It's a vicious circle, and it means more space, more filing cabinets, more disks, more archive boxes – more money!

Clutter and hazards

Records all over the place – piles and boxes and crates, on the floor, on top of cabinets and behind anything which doesn't move – create a hazardous working environment. I know of one organization which couldn't solve the problem of staff retrieving archive boxes from storage and piling them up in the walkways alongside their desks. That is, until the administration manager tripped over a box, fell and broke his leg. The next day, staff were informed that any boxes found beside desks after 6 p.m. would be removed by security staff, and that departments would be charged an amount per box to cover the cost of the extra member of staff required to provide this 'service'. Problem solved!

Security risks

If you don't know what you've got and where it is, how will you know if someone takes it and loses it, destroys it or leaks it to the press or your most threatening competitor?

The experience of many organizations in many sectors over the last thirty years shows that not managing records in a systematic, planned way can have disastrous consequences. It can result in time-consuming and costly investigations by auditors, regulators and the police. It can cost a great deal of money in fines and other penalties. It can have a devastating impact on the 'bottom line', through loss of investment and new business. It can cost an organization its reputation and even its future. It can cost its executives their careers and livelihoods.

Summary

After reading this chapter you should be aware that:

➤ organizations run on records, and can't run efficiently and effectively without them
➤ managing records means records management – systematic and consistent control of records throughout their lifecycle
➤ managing records properly brings real business benefits. Not managing them creates significant business risks.

So now you know *what* records are, and *why* it's important to manage them. The rest of this book is about *how* to manage them in general, and how to get to grips with your organization's records in particular.

Part 2
Managing records

Introduction

This part covers the essential elements of records management:

> ➢ designing and managing filing systems
> ➢ developing and implementing a retention and destruction policy
> ➢ planning and controlling storage and retrieval
> ➢ identifying and protecting vital records.

and two particularly topical issues:

> ➢ managing e-mail
> ➢ managing records through organizational upheaval.

Chapter 2
Well . . . it's only filing, isn't it?
Designing filing systems that really work

In this chapter you'll find out:

➤ **what makes a filing system a good filing system**
➤ **how to design filing systems that work**
➤ **how to make sure that they keep working.**

What is it about 'filing' that really turns people off? If you need some peace and quiet to get stuck into your reading pile or surf the Net, try calling a meeting to discuss the filing system. Let's face it, on the scale of sexy, filing is down there with filling in tax returns. And like 'a simple tax form', many people think that 'a good filing system' is a contradiction in terms. The most common complaints about filing systems are:

➤ 'It doesn't make sense.'
➤ 'It's too complicated.'
➤ 'I never know where to file things – there's either no appropriate file or several'.
➤ 'It's out of date.'
➤ 'It's full of stuff that's never used.'
➤ 'I can never find anything.'

And just in case you're thinking that I'm only talking about paper filing systems, I'm not. Given that most people like computers a lot more than they like paperwork, you might expect them to find electronic filing more exciting (or at least less boring) than paper filing, and to be better organized about it. You'd be disappointed. Electronic filing systems are often more chaotic than paper ones. So these statistics are shocking but not surprising:

> - up to 10% of staff time is spent looking for records and information
> - 45% of documents are filed in more than one place
> - 85% of documents which are filed are never retrieved.

If all this sounds familiar, there's a lot of scope for you to improve your organization's efficiency and effectiveness by setting up filing systems that really do work.

Critical success factors

Filing systems that really work have several things in common:

1 the file classification schemes reflect and support the organization's business functions and activities;
2 the physical arrangement of files reflects the file classification schemes and is 'retention-conscious';
3 the titles of files accurately reflect their contents;
4 the finding aids are based on user needs and are easy to use;
5 the use and retention of files is monitored to ensure that the systems do not become clogged up with inactive or redundant material;
6 the physical movement of hard copy files is tracked, so that files can always be located when they are needed;
7 there are clear and simple procedures for using the systems, and these are well-publicized and enforced;
8 the users have been trained to understand the systems and to follow the procedures;
9 the systems are regularly reviewed to see that they still meet the needs of the business, and to change them if they don't.

These are the things you have to get right – the critical success factors (CSFs).

File classification schemes

As an information professional, you know that the problem with all classification schemes is that they are subjective. The people who devise them think that they are logical and easy to follow, but the people who actually use them often see things differently. Think about some of the classification schemes you use every day: the *Yellow Pages* and the way supermarkets are laid out, for example. Don't some of them drive you mad? My pet hate is bookshops. I went to a branch of a well-known chain recently, looking for a copy of *Hiawatha* for my daughter. I went to the 'Children's Books' section and looked at 'Poetry'. Not there. I looked at 'Fiction' under 'L'. Not there either. I looked at 'Large books' (you never know). No. I looked in 'Classics' under 'L'. No. I went to the grown-up poetry section. Not there either. I gave up and went to the enquiry desk. When I explained what I was looking for, the assistant rolled her eyes heavenwards and led me back to 'Children's Books'. She went straight to a display stand, took out *Hiawatha* and handed it to me, with a look that said 'Haven't you ever been in a bookshop before?'. 'It's under 'Puffin'' she said, witheringly, and left. Well, excu-u-se me!

Exactly the same thing can happen to the users of a filing system.

Exercise

Figure 2.1(a) is an extract from the filing system in a small service company. Figure 2.1(b) is a list of some of the types of records generated by the company. Write the classification number which you think best applies to each records series in the right hand column of Figure 2.1(b).

Now check your answers with the actual filing system references in Figure 2.1(c) on page 174 (the page after Appendix 2).

```
2   PERSONNEL
            2.1   Recruitment
                        2.1.1  Vacancies
                        2.1.2  Temps
                        2.1.6  Milk Round
            2.2   Training
                        2.2.1  In-house
                        2.2.2  Contract
            2.3   Pensions
            2.4   Payroll
            2.5   Company Car Scheme
                        2.5.1  Renewal schedule
                        2.5.2  Insurance
                        2.5.3  Accidents

6   FACILITIES
            6.1   Health & Safety
                        6.1.1  Inspections
                        6.1.2  Accidents
            6.2   Insurance
                        6.2.1  Premises
                        6.2.2  Plant & equipment
                        6.2.3  Vehicles
            6.3   Security
                        6.3.1  Inspections
                        6.3.2  Incidents
            6.4   Services
                        6.4.1  Electricity
                        6.4.2  Gas
                        6.4.3  Water
            6.5   Maintenance
                        6.5.1  Lifts
                        6.5.2  HVAC
                        6.5.3  Boilers
                        6.5.4  Lighting
                        6.5.5  Vending machines
            6.6   Housekeeping
                        6.6.1  Office cleaning
                        6.6.2  Waste disposal
            6.7   Communications
                        6.7.1  Telephones
                        6.7.2  Pagers
```

Fig. 2.1(a) *Extract from the filing system in a small service company*

RECORDS SERIES	FILE CODE
1. Accident Reports *6.1.2*	
2. Boiler Inspection Certificates *6.5.5*	
3. Boiler Maintenance Contracts *6.5.3*	
4. Car Insurance Claims *2.8.2*	
5. Car Insurance Policies	
6. Insurance Policies	
7. Window Cleaning Schedules	
8. Maintenance Schedules	
9. Lift Service Reports	
10. Fire Drill Notifications	
11. Induction Course Materials *2.2.1*	
12. Milk Round Schedules	
13. Waste Collection Certificates	
14. Safety Audit Reports	
15. Staff Photographs	
16. Training Course Bookings	
17. Unsuccessful Applications	
18. Vehicle Accident Reports	
19. Visitors Books	
20. Minutes of the Health & Safety Committee	

Fig. 2.1(b) *Some types of records generated by a small service company*

Did you get 20 out of 20? If you didn't get them all 'right', you're not alone. This system worked well for the people who designed it, but it broke down when the company grew bigger and new staff arrived, because:

➢ the scheme didn't fit the new departmental structure
➢ there is more than one possible place to put some records, but no obvious place for others
➢ some of the terminology is confusing – technical terms, jargon, abbreviations, colloquial names.

This example highlights the three key things you need to think about in designing file classification schemes: structure, terminology and classification codes.

Structure

File classification schemes should be based on business functions and activities. *Functions* are the things that your organization has to do to achieve its corporate goals and strategies. *Activities* are the things it does to carry out its functions. Let's look at some examples to make this clearer.

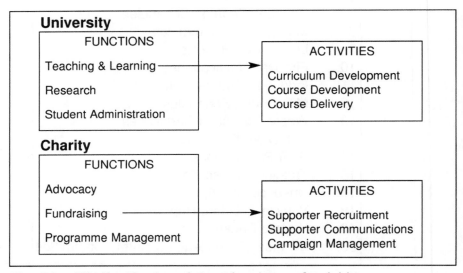

Fig. 2.2 *File classification schemes: functions and activities*

So the first thing you need to do is find out what your organization does, and how it does it, to identify the hierarchy of functions and activities which should form the basis of its classification schemes. Chapter 11 provides some guidance, but if you've never done anything like this before, you might find it helpful to get a book on basic business systems analysis or, even better, some training.

Once you've identified the hierarchy of functions and activities, you turn it into file classification schemes like this:

➢ the top level represents the function

> the second level represents the activities which make up the function

> the third and subsequent levels represent further subdivisions of the activities, if these are required, and identify specific transactions or individual entities.

Let's look at our examples again.

University		
Level 1	**Level 2**	**Level 3**
Teaching & Learning	Course Development	MA in Russian Literature

Charity			
Level 1	**Level 2**	**Level 3**	**Level 4**
Fundraising	Sponsor Recruitment	National Press Campaigns	Summer 1999

Fig. 2.3 *File classification schemes, based on hierarchy of functions and activities*

Whether your organization is a large manufacturing company or a small charity, this approach will ensure that its file classification schemes have enough categories to include all the records it generates, but only one logical category for any individual record.

A brief digression . . .

At this point, it's probably worth explaining why file classification schemes should not be based on organizational structure, because at some point you are bound to be asked. There are two reasons.

(cont.)

> **A brief digression** (continued)
>
> 1   We all know that reorganization is now a part of working life – no sooner is one reorganization completed than another one is planned. This causes havoc with filing systems which are based on the organizational structure. No sooner have the training department's files been incorporated into the personnel division's filing system than the training department is transferred to the facilities management division. By contrast, business functions and activities are fairly stable. To continue the previous example, the organization is still doing 'training'. Organizations do, of course, add new functions and activities, and drop others from time to time, but these changes are relatively easy to deal with from the point of view of filing systems. Adding or deleting whole sections of a filing scheme is relatively easy; it's splitting sections and moving the parts around that causes real problems.
>
> 2   Many business functions and activities are distributed across organizational structures. Continuing the previous example, although there is a training department, all departments maintain information about training for their own staff, so all departments need files on 'training'. If the classification scheme for training records is designed around the needs of the training department, it will not meet the needs of the other departments because it will be too detailed.

Terminology

File classification schemes should use meaningful, precise terminology. If the terminology normally used within the organization is not sufficiently meaningful and precise, you need to provide additional tools to guide users to 'preferred' terms, to get around the problems which can be caused by, for example:

> ➢ abbreviations: shortened ways of referring to words or organizations, eg M&S for Marks & Spencer

> acronyms: groups of letters to indicate groups of words, eg EXCO for Executive Committee
> synonyms: words with the same or similar meanings, eg 'human resources' and 'personnel'
> internal jargon: eg 'pinks' for 'purchase requisition copies'.

Tools can range from a simple list of the terms which are used in a classification scheme, to a thesaurus which specifies the meaning of each term and its relationships to other terms in the scheme. The acid test is 'Could a new member of staff use the file classification scheme independently on their first day?'

Classification codes

A classification code is simply shorthand for the name of a classification category. Codes are usually meaningful, ie they indicate the position of each category relative to others in the classification scheme. Let's look at one of our earlier examples which has had codes allocated to the classification categories.

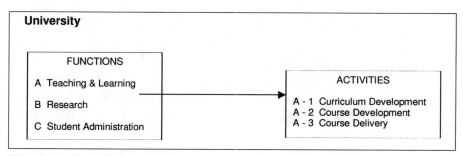

Fig. 2.4 *Classification codes*

The classification code for 'course development' is A – 2. Further subdivisions of 'course development' might be coded as A – 2 – A, A – 2 – B etc.

Codes are not always necessary or useful. They are essential in large, wide-ranging filing systems, but they may not add value in very small systems. If you do use them, keep them simple. Studies have shown that

29

most people can only reliably memorize strings of seven characters or less. Think about the combination of characters, too. The most memorable combination is 'letter – number – letter', for example 'A – 2 – A'. Strings of numbers or letters are more easily transposed, and this greatly increases the risk of misfiling.

Physical arrangement

The physical arrangement of files should be:

> ➢ logical, so that files and individual documents can be quickly located and retrieved
> ➢ retention-conscious, so that redundant or time-expired material can be easily identified and removed.

You need to think about both the physical order of files, and the arrangement of documents within files.

Files

The most logical way to arrange files is according to the file classification schemes. In paper filing systems, this means that folders are arranged in filing cabinets by classification category, either alphabetically by category title or alpha-numerically by classification code. In electronic filing systems, files are represented by directories. Directory trees should be organized to reflect the classification scheme as accurately as possible. Fig. 2.5 is an example from a Windows directory tree. The four-digit number after the 'A – 2 – A' is the official Course Code.

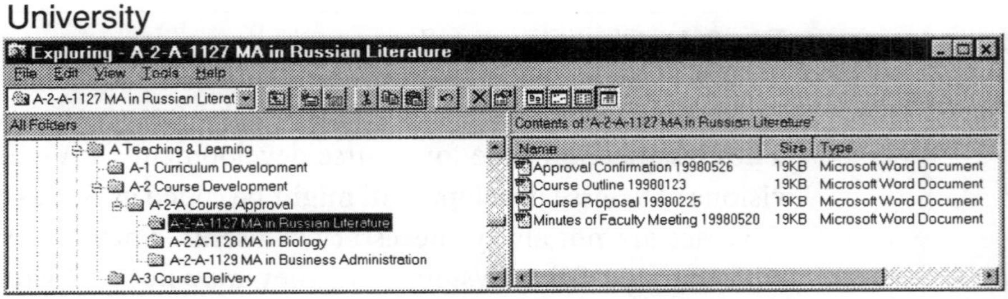

University

Fig. 2.5 *Windows Explorer screen print*

The two golden rules for organizing files within classification categories are:

1 Separate records from reference materials:
   Records must be retained in line with the established retention policy. Reference material should not be scheduled for retention (see Chapter 3) and can be disposed of as soon as it's no longer useful.
2 Separate policy files from operational files:
   Policy files generally have longer retention periods than operational files.

Documents within files

There are no hard and fast rules for arranging documents within files, but a logical arrangement is usually fairly obvious. For example:

➢ correspondence and meeting papers are usually arranged in date order
➢ invoices are usually arranged numerically by invoice number, or by date
➢ bank statements are usually arranged by account number
➢ reports are usually arranged by report number.

Generally speaking, the users of files should decide which arrangement best meets their retrieval needs. The important thing is that there is a defined order which is applied consistently.

A 'special case'

Case files contain different types of documents which all relate to one individual person or thing – for example, an employee, a supplier, a building – and which need to be kept together for ease of reference and use. For example:

➢ employee files in a personnel department
➢ supplier files in a purchasing department
➢ client files in a consulting company

31

> building files in a property management department
> patient files in a hospital
> project files in an architect's practice.

Some of the documents in these files may have only short-term significance, while others may have considerable long-term value. Taking a function-activity approach to developing a file classification scheme often means that case files fit into more than one classification category. What should you do?

> You could put the files in one classification category and give users specific instructions on where to find them. This can work – it depends on the users.
> You could duplicate the files and put each copy into each 'correct' classification category. This is not practical for fairly obvious reasons – time, money and space for copying, filing and storage.

And neither of these options is 'retention-conscious'. Putting different types of documents in one sequence in one file means that

> either the whole file must be kept for the lifetime of the most valuable document in it. This means that documents which have only short-term value will be kept beyond their useful life, taking up space which could be better used and possibly creating business risks for the organization (see Chapter 3).
> or the file will need to be weeded to remove redundant material. Weeding is a very time-consuming process and most people would rather settle down to their tax returns. In an electronic filing system, it's a nightmare.

So what's the alternative? You could physically split the files and put the separate parts into the correct classification categories. This is technically correct but it is not usually practical – filing and retrieval is more time-consuming, and users need several files rather than just one to do their work. The answer is to divide the files into separate sections, each with its own classification code and retention period, but to file them physically together in a separate sequence, ie separate from the 'routine' files which are arranged according to the file classification scheme. In a paper filing system, this means a separate sequence of folders for case files, arranged in the most logical order, for example:

➢ project files by project number
➢ staff files by employee name or number
➢ customer files by company name or account number.

In an electronic filing system, it means separate directories for case files. Let's look at an example.

University Purchasing Department
The Purchasing Department maintains a Supplier File for every approved supplier. The file is opened when the supplier is approved and closed when their contract is terminated. Each file contains many different types of documents, eg

- Supplier Evaluation Report
- Supplier Authorisation
- Supplier Contract
- Correspondence about routine matters and important contractual issues
- Notes of meetings, both planned reviews and ad hoc meetings to deal with problems
- Copies of Purchase Orders
- Supplier Contract Review Reports

Originally, paper documents were filed, in date order, in a folder for each supplier. These folders were bulky and difficult to use. They became dog-eared and documents were damaged. Electronic documents were filed in a directory for each supplier, but were difficult to retrieve because there was no file structure and no rules for naming documents. Retrieval was time-consuming and documents were frequently lost.

When the filing system was redesigned, the Supplier Files clearly fitted under the Level 1 (Function) category 'Procurement'. However, they contained documents relating to four Level 2 (Activity) categories – Supplier Approval, Contract Management, Purchasing and Supplier Administration. The solution was to split each Supplier File into four separate sections like this:

(cont.)

33

University Purchasing Department (continued)

1. Supplier Approval, containing:
    – Supplier Evaluation Report
    – Supplier Authorisation
    – related correspondence, notes of meetings and other documents
2. Contract Management, containing:
    – Supplier Contract
    – Supplier Contract Review Reports
    – related correspondence, notes of meetings and other documents
3. Purchasing, containing:
    – copies of Purchase Orders
    – related correspondence and other documents
4. Supplier Administration, containing:
    – Documents relating to routine matters such as holidays, office closures,
      packaging etc.

They were filed under 'Procurement', like this:

M Procurement

    Supplier
    Files

        Alphafactors
        plc

            M-1 Supplier Approval
            M-2 Supplier Administration
            M-3 Contract Management
            M-4 Purchasing

        Countrywide
        Couriers plc

            M-1 Supplier Approval
            M-2 Supplier Administration
            M-3 Contract Management
            M-4 Purchasing

        Delia's
        Delicatessen

            M-1 Supplier Approval
            M-2 Supplier Administration
            M-3 Contract Management
            M-4 Purchasing

To make things easy for the users, files were given colour-coded labels. All M-1 Supplier Approval files had green labels, all M-4 Purchasing Files had blue labels, and so on.

(cont.)

University Purchasing Department (continued)

The electronic filing system was structured in the same way, using separate directories for the four sections, like this:

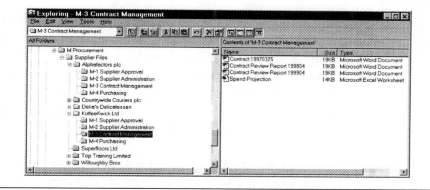

File titles

File titles

> ➢ should accurately reflect the contents of the files. Be as specific as possible. Indicate both the information content and the types of documents, for example 'Personnel committee – agenda & minutes' rather than just 'Personnel committee'.
> ➢ should be meaningful. Don't use words like 'General' (= 'Don't know') and 'Miscellaneous' (= 'Can't be bothered to think about it'). If you wouldn't use it as an index term, don't use it as a file title.
> ➢ should be as simple and short as possible. If, to be meaningful and accurately reflect the contents, the title is too long (say more than five or six words), consider splitting it into two or more files, either by content or by document type, e.g. have three files:
> – Personnel committee: agenda & submitted documents
> – Personnel committee: minutes & action points
> – Personnel committee: correspondence
> instead of one:

– Personnel committee – agenda & submitted documents, minutes, correspondence, action points.

Finding aids

Finding aids, in the form of topical lists and indexes, enable users to identify and retrieve records across classification categories, a key requirement for team-based working and in knowledge-based organizations. They can be manual lists, card indexes or computer databases. What really matters is that they are up to date and well organized, and contain sufficient detail to allow users to identify and locate relevant records quickly. The key things to think about are:

> the level at which finding aids should operate: container level (for example a file, a storage box) or item level (for example a single document, a tape)
> whether indexing terms should be controlled or not. Indexing terms may be restricted to terms used in the file classification scheme, or taken from the content of key records, or completely unrestricted.

Computer systems can take much of the hard work out of indexing, and a wide range of systems is available. Here are a couple of examples.

University
All documents generated by third-party funded research projects are managed in a document management system (RDMS). Third-party documents are scanned and the images are stored on optical disks. Internally generated documents are stored in an electronic filing system on the university's network servers. They are all indexed in the RDMS. The document management system has several controlled index fields which are linked to pull-down lists, from which terms are manually selected. The system also builds a cumulative index from the text of internally generated documents.

On the other hand, where user needs are predictable and relatively simple, a system which enables manual entry or selection of key terms, can be equally if not more effective.

International aid charity
All files in the fundraising, emergency response and programme development departments are indexed by 'Country Name' and 'Category' so that managers can immediately access files relating to contact with particular countries, or work of particular types, or both. The files are listed in a simple database which has two index fields, both of which are linked to controlled pull-down lists from which terms can be selected.

To make the most of records as information resources, indexes to files should be integrated as far as possible with other indexes in the organization. If someone wants to know about 'Poland', they may want to know about records relating to Poland as well as third-party materials in the library, and they may want to know about electronic files as well as those in hard copy.

Monitoring the use and retention of files

The use of individual files must be monitored so that files which are not active, but which need to be retained, can be transferred to inactive storage or archives. In paper filing systems, use is monitored by file tracking systems (see Chapter 6), although of course the data will only be accurate if the systems are actually *used*. Electronic filing systems automatically monitor use of individual directories and documents.

It's also vital to make sure that time-expired files are promptly removed from filing systems. Each file or directory should be given a retention period or a review date in accordance with the established records retention policy (see Chapter 3). This information should then be stored in a 'bring forward' system, so that on any given date it's possible to see which files are due for review or destruction. 'Bring forward' systems range from simple index cards to computer databases to 'automatic archiving' options in software applications.

Tracking the physical movement of hard copy files

Systems for tracking the physical movement of files are described in Chapter 6, *Managing Active Records*.

Procedures

Managing a bad filing system won't make it a good filing system, but not managing a good filing system will make it a bad one, so there must be clear and simple procedures for:

 ➢ adding and removing classification categories
 ➢ updating finding aids
 ➢ opening and closing files
 ➢ filing documents
 ➢ retrieving and returning files.

The same procedures must apply to both paper and electronic filing systems, but there will obviously be differences in *how* they are applied. In paper systems which are accessed directly by users, you have to rely on them to do what they've been asked to do, and not to do what they've been asked not to do. In electronic systems, some controls are easier to enforce because you can use the technology to 'make' people do things that they should do, and 'stop' them from doing things they shouldn't do.

Adding and removing classification categories

It's essential to control changes to the file classification scheme, to prevent duplicate or unnecessary categories being created, and to make sure that those which are no longer relevant to the business are removed.

The most effective way to do this is to route all requests for changes through one person who has been trained to understand the structure of the system, and to advise users on how to use it. If a new category is justified, this person is responsible for setting it up and updating the finding aids. If a category is to be removed, he or she is responsible for making sure that the records in the redundant category are reclassified or removed from the system, and for updating the finding aids.

Specially designed forms are normally used to request changes to file classification schemes. You'll have to make sure that all users understand the procedures for requesting the addition or removal of classification categories, and you'll then have to rely on them to follow the procedures. In an electronic system, it's easier to control because you can prevent users from creating or deleting directories.

Finding aids

It's obviously vital that finding aids are kept up to date. Whatever form they take, they should be controlled and updated regularly, ideally by someone who really understands both the classification scheme and the business.

Opening and closing files

The opening of new files must be controlled, to avoid the creation of duplicate or unnecessary files and to ensure that:

- ➢ new files are correctly classified
- ➢ correct retention periods are assigned
- ➢ finding aids are updated with the details.

Closing of files must also be controlled, to ensure that files are not closed by one person to be immediately re-opened by another, and that finding aids are promptly updated to indicate closed files. The most effective way to control the creation and closure of files is to have one person who is responsible for doing it. Again, this is 'easier' in an electronic system because you can prevent users from creating or deleting directories.

Filing documents

Filing must be controlled to ensure that:

> ➤ only documents which should be filed are filed – the filing system must not become a dumping ground for useless or unnecessary records
> ➤ documents are properly classified.

First, it must be clear which documents are to be filed in the filing system, and which are not. While it can be difficult to be specific about which documents should be filed, it's fairly easy to come up with a list of the kinds of documents which definitely shouldn't be filed, to avoid the system becoming clogged up with trivia and duplicates. Here are some examples:

> ➤ 'transmission' documents which add nothing to the document which they accompanied, e.g. fax covers which say 'Here is the document' or 'As discussed earlier' and memos which say 'Please let me have your comments on the attached'
> ➤ itineraries, after completion of journeys
> ➤ correspondence regarding bookings of restaurant tables
> ➤ 'CC' and 'FYI' copies of documents.

If the system includes both paper and electronic documents, it must be clear what gets filed where. For example:

> ➤ should electronic documents be printed and filed in the paper files?
> ➤ *and* filed in the electronic files?

Next, it must be clear who is responsible for classifying documents. Should it be:

> ➤ users? Ideally. The people who generate documents are the best qualified to make these decisions, *provided that* they have been trained to understand and use the filing system.

> ➤ dedicated filing staff? Only if they have been trained to understand the organization's business.
> ➤ both? No – this is a recipe for disaster. It's one or the other, I'm afraid.

Who is responsible for actually filing documents? Provided that documents have been classified correctly, anyone can actually file them. One very important point: if users are responsible for classifying, and filing staff are responsible for filing, users must have clear instructions on how to mark documents with the classification codes. For example,

When you have decided where a document should be filed, write the classification code in the top right-hand corner of the document.

or, in an electronic system,

When you have decided where a document should be filed, type the classification code in the footer.

Hard copy filing procedures should also make it clear how documents are to be physically filed, for example:

> ➤ are unbound documents to be punched/stapled/clipped/inserted in plastic wallets?
> ➤ are bound documents to be punched or stored separately?

Filing procedures for electronic documents must specify how documents are to be named. Let's face it, 'John.doc' is not particularly helpful. I've seen one electronic filing system containing more than 500 documents which were named 'JHW001.doc' to 'JHW5....doc'. 'I can't find anything – it's a hopeless system', said the secretary concerned. Quite. So document naming rules are essential. The same rules apply as for file titles – document names should accurately reflect the contents of the document, and they should be meaningful and as short as possible. This is a challenge if the IT system only allows eight-character document names. The best option here is to use the eight characters to give the document a unique code which is explained in a separate list or index. On the other hand, if the system allows 256-character document names, the only problem may be keeping them sufficiently brief. The naming rules should make it clear what the document name must include (for example date, author, recipient, document type, client name, project number) and in what format. For example,

> ➤ should dates be American style (month/day/year), Japanese style (year/month/day) or British style (day/month/year)?
> ➤ should personal names be in the form 'surname, first name' or 'surname, initials'?

Finally, the fewer people who do filing, the more consistently accurate the filing will be.

Retrieving files

The most common complaint about filing systems is that they don't work because 'people just walk off with things'. Tracking systems will be discussed more fully in Chapter 6, but in the end, whether any tracking system works effectively depends *entirely* on the users.

You can only put good systems in place and get management to support you in your efforts to get people to use them.

Maintenance of hard copy files

Frequently used files can get very bulky. Punched holes tear and documents fall out. Labels fall off. Tatty files aren't pleasant or easy to use, and documents are more likely to be lost. They don't reflect well on the department or the organization if they're taken to meetings. So someone must be responsible for replacing damaged file covers, labels and so on.

Making it easy

Whatever procedures you set up, they must be enforced by whatever means are available or appropriate. This may sound harsh, but there is no excuse for anyone, however senior, ignoring or refusing to comply with simple procedures designed to control the organization's records and make life easier for everyone. Of course, presenting this message in the right way is half the battle, and having strong management support is very important. *Simple* is the key word. The simpler the procedure, the more likely it is that people will follow it, and the more cussed they will appear if they don't. Making it easy for people to do what they have to do is the name of the game, so here are some things to think about.

1 If you want people to fill in forms, they must be short and easy to complete, and supplies of blanks must be readily available. If you can make the forms electronic, available as standard document templates or on an intranet, even better.

2 When you are writing instructions and procedures, remember to look at things from the user's point of view. It's always better to give step-by-step instructions, and to have more simple steps rather than fewer complicated ones. Get a friendly user to check a draft for your assumptions and quantum leaps.

3 Providing additional resources may be the most cost-effective way to get something done. Take filing, for example. Files are only worth having if they are complete and up to date. Files are only up to date if new documents are filed promptly and accurately. But most users hate filing and, frankly, aren't very good at it. In any case, filing is not the best use of their time unless it is formally part of their job – calculate what they cost an hour if you are in any doubt. So having someone whose job it is to collect and file documents may be the most cost-effective solution.

User training

You must train users to understand the system and to follow the procedures set out for using and maintaining the system. For some tips on how to achieve this, see Chapter 13.

Review

Finally, you must review filing systems regularly to make sure that they continue to reflect and support the business they serve, to incorporate developments in professional standards or best practice, or simply to make changes in the light of experience. A cooperative effort between those responsible for 'policing' the system – you? – and its regular users will get the best results.

Summary

➤ Filing systems can really work!

➤ Having good filing systems for electronic records is just as important as having good filing systems for paper and other records.

➤ A good filing system reflects and supports what the organization does and how it does it, and is regularly reviewed to make sure that it stays relevant and up to date.

➤ Managing a bad filing system won't make it a good filing system, but not managing a good filing system will make it a bad one.

➤ Make it easy for users to do what they have to do to keep the filing system working.

Chapter 3
How long is a piece of string?
Keeping records for as long as you need
them – and no longer

In this chapter you'll find out:

➤ how to decide which records to retain, and for how long
➤ who should make the decisions
➤ how to make sure that retention *policy* becomes retention *practice*.

Every organization needs a records retention policy. Most people aren't
well informed about legal or regulatory requirements to retain records –
after all, why should they be? – but nearly everybody has opinions about
how long records should be kept, based on their experiences or on their
instincts. So if there's no formal policy to follow, individual managers
and staff do what they think best. Some of them hoard records, afraid to
throw anything away, while others throw out records that 'they' don't
need any more at the earliest opportunity. Sometimes, important records
which should be kept get thrown away, and junk which should be
thrown away gets kept. If this never causes a problem for the organization, it's by good luck rather than good management.

If your organization doesn't want to rely on luck, it must have a clear
records retention policy and make sure that everyone understands and
uses it. There are three key issues to deal with in establishing a policy:

1 How long should records be kept?
2 Who should make retention decisions?
3 How should the decisions be documented and communicated
   within the organization?

How long should records be kept?

Records should be kept for as long as they are needed to meet operational needs and legal and regulatory requirements. 'Thanks a lot!' you may say, 'How long is that?' Well, how long is a piece of string? Sorry, but there are very few hard and fast rules and very few easy answers. Each group of records in your organization needs to be assessed individually, to:

> ➢ determine its value as a source of *information* about the business and its operations, relationships and environment
> ➢ assess its importance as *evidence* of business activities and decisions
> ➢ establish whether there are any *legal or regulatory retention requirements*, and assess the relative risks of non-compliance.

Information

Identifying records which contain important information sounds simple, doesn't it? It's not. Importance is relative. To assess the information value of records, you need to understand the business process that generated them, and the importance of the records to that process. Then you need to consider whether the information they contain is unique or widely available, and the cost of replacing it if it was lost (the cost of re-inventing the wheel). You may also need to take account of factors outside the organization. The information may be important to others, for different purposes, over long periods of time. For example, some of the records about current ground-breaking research into genetically-modified foods will be extremely valuable to scientists in the future. However, there are some traps to avoid. Don't assume that:

1 Only things done by important people are important. Do you care about a minor, relatively insignificant project ten years ago just because the then project manager is now the Chairman of the BBC or the Prime Minister?

2 Only things which were done are significant. Things which *weren't* done may be just as significant. For example, architectural partner-

ships don't need to retain design records for structures which were never built. However, most do because these records contain the ideas and embedded expertise of their designers, and they may be valuable sources for future designs.

3 Only things which were successful are significant. Again, the architect's practice is likely to retain design and construction records for longer than required by law. These are the only sources of information about what went right, what went wrong, what turned out well and what turned out badly. These are invaluable resources for future projects.

4 If you keep anything for long enough, you'll find a use for it. My first professional job involved sorting out abandoned records in a closed office building. Among all the records piled up in filing cabinets, cupboards and store rooms, most of which obviously hadn't been looked at in years, I found lots of stationery, including a brown envelope containing little bits of string. The envelope was marked 'String (too short)'. We all know the truth about this one: don't keep anything 'just in case'.

Evidence

Every business process has an 'audit trail'. The records which document or form part of that 'audit trail' provide the evidence of what was done, why, when, where and by whom. Figure 3.1 is a simple example which indicates the key records in a typical recruitment process.

Legal and regulatory requirements

To assess the impact of legal and regulatory requirements, and to assess the relative risks of non-compliance, you need to understand your organization's compliance environment. First, you need to identify the laws and regulations which apply to your organization and its business. Start by looking at generic laws and regulations which apply to all organizations which do particular things. For example:

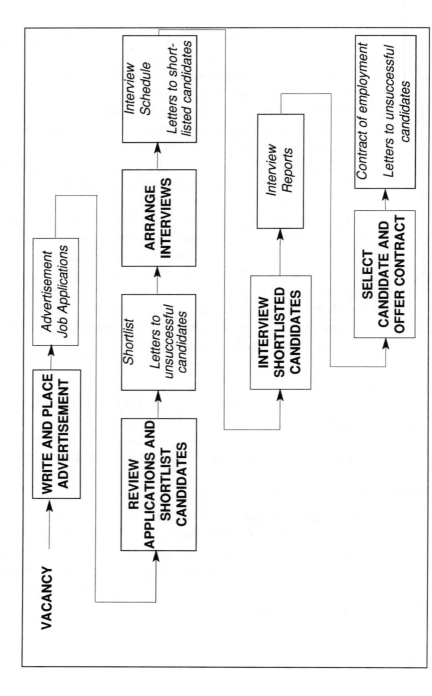

Fig. 3.1 *Key records in a typical recruitment process*

1 *If your organization occupies business premises*, it must comply with local authority regulations regarding, for example, planning controls, fire protection, noise and nuisance.

2 *If your organization pays taxes*, it must comply with the Taxes Management Act 1970 (amended annually by the Finance Act), Inland Revenue regulations and Customs and Excise rules.

3 *If your organization employs staff*, it must comply with legislation and associated regulations on:
   - discrimination, eg Race Relations Act 1976, Disability Discrimination Act 1995
   - employment rights, eg Employment Rights Act 1996, Employment Rights (Dispute Resolution) Act 1998
   - wages, eg National Minimum Wage Act 1998 and The National Minimum Wage Regulations 1999
   - health and safety, eg Health and Safety at Work Act 1974 and the Workplace Health, Safety and Welfare Regulations 1992.

   Depending on the type of work involved, it may also need to comply with additional measures for example Personal Protective Equipment at Work Regulations 1992, Control of Substances Hazardous to Health (Amendment) Regulations 1997, Control of Asbestos at Work Regulations 1987, Display Screen Equipment Regulations 1992.

Next, consider what type of organization it is, and what laws and regulations may apply to the way it conducts it business. For example: limited companies must comply with the Companies Acts; charities must comply with The Charities Act. Then look at sector-specific laws and regulations. Here are some examples.

1 *Companies which develop and market pharmaceutical products* must comply with the requirements of the Medicines Control Agency in the UK, and with similar authorities in other countries in which they manufacture or market products, such as the Food and Drugs Administration in the United States.

2 *Organizations which offer financial services* must comply with, for example, the Financial Services Act 1986 and the Money Laundering Regulations 1993. They are regulated by the Financial Services Authority and must take account of its requirements.

3 *Privatized utilities* must comply with the decisions of their respective regulatory bodies, for example, OFWAT, OFGAS, OFTEL.

Here are some suggestions to help you to get started with your research.

1 Establish good working relationships with functional and operational managers. They are normally familiar with legal and regulatory requirements in their specific fields. (If they're not, the organization has more to worry about than not having a records retention policy!) They may be able to provide the information you need. If not, they should be able to point you to other sources of information or contacts, and you may be able to take advantage of their memberships of professional bodies to get access to specialist libraries or information services.

2 Ditto for your organization's professional advisers.

3 Most regulatory organizations and professional bodies have Web sites which either provide useful information about compliance issues or provide contact points for more information.

4 The HMSO website (**http://www.hmso.gov.uk/**) is an excellent source of information about legislation and contains the full-text of all Statutory Instruments published since 1 January 1997.

5 Legal publications by, for example, Butterworths and Croner provide topical summaries of, and guidance on, legislation and regulations. Catalogues are available on their websites.

When you've identified all the relevant laws and regulations, you need to study each one to find out whether

1 it expressly requires you to retain a specific record for a specific period of time;

2 it expressly requires you to retain specific information for a specific period of time;

3 it implies that you should retain records or information of a particular kind for a particular period of time, because you could be the subject of an investigation or a party to legal proceedings within that period.

If it's 1, it should be fairly simple to relate the specific requirement to your organization's records, and to identify which ones need to be retained for the prescribed period. If it's 2, there may be several groups of records which contain the information, and it will be a case of selecting the most complete or reliable one. In either case, the risk management decision will be limited to assessing the severity of the penalties for non-compliance. However, if it's 3, the risk management decision is more complex. Someone will need to make an informed judgment about:

> the likelihood of legal proceedings or other events which may require the production of particular records
> the likely penalties for the organization if it could not produce these records
> the likely costs of retaining the records for the full period of time in which proceedings could arise.

The corporate culture will have a significant influence on this decision. The organization's perception of itself – 'leading edge', 'conservative', 'innovative', 'reliable' – and of how others see it, will influence its approach to retaining records. Sometimes it's predictable – conservative organizations take a conservative approach, keeping more records for longer periods. However, interestingly, organizations which see themselves as being at the 'leading edge' are often more conservative about record-keeping than their more 'conservative' competitors.

A brief digression . . .

. . . into the minefield of limitation periods, the subject of the most popular myth about records retention. Briefly, the law places a limitation on the periods within which legal proceedings of various kinds can be brought. In England and Wales, the Limitation Act 1980 (as amended) applies. In Scotland, it's the Prescription and Limitation (Scotland) Act 1973. For Northern Ireland, see the Statute of Limitations (Northern Ireland) 1958, the Limitation Act (Northern Ireland) 1964 and the Limitation Amendment (Northern Ireland) Order 1982. When most people talk about 'legal requirements' to retain records, limitation periods are often what they're thinking about. In fact, these pieces of legislation make no specific mention of records at all. In simple terms, they specify the periods within which you can bring, or be subject to, legal proceedings of various kinds, such as actions for damages for breach of contract. Each organization must decide for itself how likely it is to become involved in such proceedings, and the implications of this for retention of its records. In other words, how likely is it that someone will bring an action against the organization, and if they do, does the organization want the records or would it rather they had been destroyed? Have a look at the Turner & Newall case in Appendix 2 if you haven't already done so.

Retention periods

Retention periods should be clearly expressed so that there can be no confusion about what is meant. Periods of time should be specific – days, weeks, months, years. In the case of years, it may be necessary to distinguish between 'calendar year', 'financial year' and 'tax year'. It should also be clearly stated when the period of time starts to run. Here are a few examples (not recommendations!) to make this clearer:

> ➢ termination of employment + 6 years for staff files
> ➢ current financial year + 6 years for purchase invoices
> ➢ current year + 2 years for security incident reports
> ➢ completion of book + 1 year for visitors books.

Codes are normally used for common periods or events, for example CFY = current financial year, CTY = current tax year, S = settlement, AU = audit. If you decide to use them, make sure that they are listed, with their meanings, on whatever documentation you produce (see page 54).

Who should decide how long records should be kept?

Deciding how long to retain records is mostly a matter of judgment and risk management. Whoever makes the decisions must understand the purpose and importance of the records in question, be well-informed on the issues and the risks associated with retaining or destroying them and have the authority to commit the organization to the potential consequences of the decision. In practical terms, this usually means that several people, or groups of people, must be involved:

> ➤ functional and operational managers and staff can advise on operational needs for information and evidence of business activities and processes
> ➤ professional advisers – lawyers, accountants, tax advisers, auditors and compliance officers – can advise on legal and regulatory requirements, and on standards and best practice
> ➤ information professionals (that's you!) can look at the information/knowledge value of the records from a 'whole organization' perspective
> ➤ senior executives – the board, the executive committee or whatever the most formal group of senior management is called – must make the final decisions because they are ultimately responsible and accountable for managing the organization's assets and liabilities.

As an information professional, you're in an excellent position to co-ordinate the decision-making process. Your other responsibilities probably mean that if you've been in the organization for any length of time, you understand the business and how it works and you have lots of contacts. You also have one other essential skill – you know how to find out what people need to know to make the decisions.

Documenting the decisions

Records retention decisions must be properly documented. Yes, you need to create more records – and decide how long to keep them! You need to produce two types of document: the Records Retention Authority and the Records Retention Schedule.

Records Retention Authority

This is the formal record of retention decisions – the policy document. It should contain details of each records series, the agreed retention period for each one, and the rationale for that retention period, including full citations for legal and regulatory requirements. It must be authorized by the managers responsible for making the retention decisions, and by the senior executive who is ultimately responsible for the policy. Figure 3.2 is an example. Note that codes are used to describe the point at which the retention period starts to run. This keeps the documentation compact.

Records Retention Schedule

This is the working summary of the retention decisions. The Schedule sets out the lifecycle for each records series, including what should happen to it at the end of its retention period. Figure 3.3 is an example.

Everyone in the organization who handles records – ie everyone – must have access to the Schedule and be able to use it, so it must be easy to find and easy to use. Distribution of paper copies is OK, but publishing it on an intranet is even better, particularly in large organizations. Individuals may only deal with a few categories of records and would otherwise have to rummage through a large paper document to find the retention periods they need. If paper schedules are your only option, consider producing separate functional or departmental schedules or an alphabetical index of records series.

| DIVISION | DEPARTMENT | DEPARTMENT CODE |
| Finance | Accounting | F229 |

Series	Operational		Legal / Regulatory		Total
	Retention Period	Reason	Retention Period	Citation	Retention Period
Purchase Invoices	CFY + 1	Supplier queries; Audit	CFY + 6	Value Added Tax Act 1994	CFY + 6

AUTHORIZATION

OPERATIONS	LEGAL & COMPLIANCE	EXECUTIVE
Name T Beaker	Name G Black	Name C Bunn
Signature	Signature	Signature
Position Manager, Accounting	Position Compliance Officer	Position Financial Controller

Fig. 3.2 *Records Retention Authority*

DIVISION		DEPARTMENT					DEPARTMENT CODE	
Finance		Accounting					F229	
Series		Official copy				Other copies		Notes
	Department Code	On-site	Off-site	Total	Action	Retention	Action	
Purchase Invoices	F229	CFY+1	5	CFY+6	D	CFY	D	

Fig. 3.3 *Records Retention Schedule*

Implementing the policy

Now that you've got an approved policy, you need to do just two more things. First, make sure it happens. It can be far more damaging to have a retention policy which is misused or ignored than it is not to have a policy at all – see the example in Appendix 2 again. So what can you do? Well, obviously make sure that everybody knows about the Records Retention Schedule and has access to a copy of it. Use whatever internal communication channels are available: in-house magazines, team briefings etc. If you have internal auditors or compliance departments, ask them to include 'compliance with the Records Retention Schedule' in their audits or inspections. Secondly, keep it up to date. Remember that an out-of-date retention policy is a dangerous retention policy. You must monitor legal and regulatory developments which might affect your organization and amend the retention policy as required, and promptly. Make sure that amendments are made in the same way as the original periods were agreed when the policy was first developed. Don't fall into the trap of thinking that all the hard work has been done and anyone can just make changes as required. And remember to update the Records Retention Schedules and do everything you can to make sure that staff only have access to the latest version. Obviously, this is one good reason for publishing it electronically, particularly if you can stop people printing off copies to keep in their files!

Summary

➤ Keep records for only as long as they have positive value.
➤ Decisions on records retention must be made by senior executives who can commit the organization to the potential consequences of the decisions.
➤ Deciding what to keep and how long to keep it for is mostly a matter of judgment, rarely a matter of fact.
➤ It can be more damaging to have a records retention policy which is misused, ignored or out of date than it is not to have one at all.

Chapter 4
Sorry, there wasn't time to switch off the light!
Protecting vital records

> **In this chapter you'll find out:**
>
> ➤ **what vital records are**
> ➤ **how to identify them**
> ➤ **how to protect them.**

On Saturday, 15 June 1996, an IRA bomb exploded near the Corn Exchange in the centre of Manchester. The blast devastated buildings within a one-mile radius. One company which had offices in the Corn Exchange was Carcanet Press, the poetry publishing house. Carcanet staff were able to get into the building on the following Tuesday but could only take out what they could carry with them. The same day, the building was condemned by health and safety officials. It was another three months before demolition contractors could get in to recover other property, including records. It only took Carcanet a week to get up and running again in temporary offices, but the business was seriously affected by the loss of virtually all of their records. The company's finance director was quoted in *The Independent* : 'We had 25 years of records in the Corn Exchange offices . . . everything we needed to run the business.' The company had to wait for people to chase up unpaid bills and had to reconstruct their files from copies of records held by clients and others. Carcanet was not alone. Dozens of companies were in this position. It was the same story after the London Docklands bombing, also in 1996, and the earlier Baltic Exchange and Bishopsgate attacks.

Fortunately, terrorist attacks don't happen very often, but natural disasters are more common than you might think, and they can have a devastating impact on an organization and its records. Remember the storms which devastated the South of England in October 1987? And the Easter floods which affected large areas of the Midlands in 1998? Many organizations lost a lot of records and had to spend a considerable amount of time and money recovering from the loss. Fires are even more common. In fact, all sorts of incidents can result in the loss of critical records and information, causing major disruption to business – or worse. A recent survey found that 43% of businesses which lose significant amounts of key information in a disaster go out of business within six months. Just think about it. In the immediate aftermath of a disaster, organizations need records to make insurance claims, to pay suppliers and employees, to collect money they are owed, to enforce contracts, and, of course, to resume normal operations. If they can't do these things they will certainly lose revenue. They might also lose customers, business and their reputations. If they survive this, the long-term effects can still be very serious. It can take an organization years to recover from the loss of key proprietary information and other records containing its accumulated knowledge and experience.

So identifying and protecting vital records must be seen as an investment in the form of insurance. Like all insurance, it costs money and there are few immediate tangible benefits. You have to balance the cost against the probability of disasters which could result in the loss of key records, the consequent financial or other losses and the cost of recovery. And you have to remember that learning from other organizations' mistakes is a lot less painful and expensive than learning from your own.

Identifying vital records

Vital records are the ones which, in the event of a disaster, are *essential* to maintain business continuity, which means:

> ➢ continuing or resuming operations
> ➢ recreating the legal and financial status of the organization

> ➤ preserving the rights of the organization and fulfilling its obligations to its stakeholders.

Some things just don't matter that much

If you ask departmental managers which of their records are vital for business recovery, they are likely to say – everything, or nearly everything. So, you need to start with senior executives who can take a long, hard and dispassionate look at the organization and its business, to identify vital business functions and activities. Some things that go on in the organization, even some whole departments, will not be vital. If the business suffered a major disaster, they wouldn't be on the business resumption priority list. You need to be able to discount these and focus on the functions and activities that would be on the list – these are the vital ones, and these are the ones that generate the vital records.

'Important' isn't the same as 'vital'

> ### Think about it . . .
>
> If the fire bell rang NOW, would you take any records with you as you rushed to the fire escape? (Yes, I know what the fire brigade instructions are, but just suspend disbelief for a moment.) The chances are that if you grabbed anything, it would be something on your desk, because (a) you can grab it quickly and (b) it's what's most immediately important. But even if everyone in the building grabbed what was on their desk before they left the building, the organization might still not survive, because being able to complete today's work is not the same as being able to recreate the organization and its work from scratch. Most vital records in most organizations are not on desks – they are on computers and in cabinets or storerooms. Even if it was announced that a bomb warning had been received and that everyone had to be out of the building in ten minutes, it's extremely unlikely that all of your organization's vital records could be retrieved and taken out.

Your organization won't be able to survive and recover from a disaster with just any old records, even those relating to vital functions and activities. Surviving and thriving will depend on having the *right* records. Some records are obviously vital but, as with establishing retention periods, it's mostly a matter of risk management and there are no easy answers. You need to assess the relative value of each records series to the business. If you've already established retention schedules using the methodology outlined in Chapter 3, you're halfway there. Records which have long retention periods are more likely to be vital than those which do not. However, records which have a very short life can be vital for that time, so resist the temptation to cut corners. Look at each records series and ask some critical questions. The decision tree (Figure 4.1) will get you started.

Just one word of warning here from the Carcanet example. Your organization shouldn't count on being able to get copies of records from third parties. The Inland Revenue may not be willing to provide you with copies of your tax records, and asking your customers or suppliers for copies from their files may undermine their confidence in your business at a critical time. Generally speaking, if key records couldn't be recreated from within your organization, or by obtaining copies from your professional advisers such as lawyers and auditors, you should designate them as vital.

Like all other records, vital records may be in any medium or format. They may be active or inactive. They may even have been transferred for preservation as historical archives. Generally, vital records will represent about 5% of all the records generated within the organization, depending on the nature of the business. It can be as little as 3% and as much as 10%, but if your initial estimate is well outside this range, think about it again.

Let's look at some examples of vital records.

University

➢ student database
➢ course development files
➢ research project files.

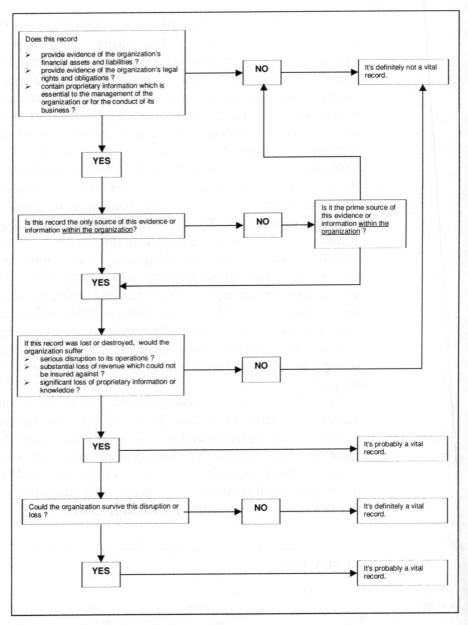

Fig. 4.1 *Vital records decision tree*

> **Pharmaceutical company, drug development division**
>
> ➢ patent files
> ➢ product development project files
> ➢ product formulation database.

> **Charity, fundraising department**
>
> ➢ donor database
> ➢ corporate supporter files
> ➢ aid programme files.

Whatever and wherever they are, vital records need to be identified and protected. Before you can protect anything, you need to establish what you're protecting it *from*. This will be covered in Chapter 5.

Protecting vital records

There are two ways of protecting vital records: duplication and dispersal, and secure storage.

Duplication and dispersal

Duplication and dispersal simply means making a copy of a record and storing the copy and the original in different locations, sufficiently far away from each other that it is extremely unlikely that both the original and the copy could be simultaneously destroyed.

Paper documents can be duplicated by:

➢ photocopying, producing a paper copy
➢ microfilming, producing a microfilm roll or fiche copy
➢ scanning, producing a digital copy.

Electronic documents can be duplicated by:

➢ printing, producing a paper copy

> ➢ producing computer output microfiche (COM) copies
> ➢ copying to another disk/tape.

Duplicating records which are not documents can be more complicated. Sometimes only one of something is normally produced, and producing another one would be very time-consuming or expensive. Sometimes duplication is simply not possible, in which case secure storage is the only option.

Duplication sounds like a very expensive option – increasing production costs by 100% – and it can be tricky to obtain management approval. The first thing you need to find out is whether you would need to start from 'scratch', or whether records are already duplicated, formally, as part of normal operations. For example, copies of records generated on a manufacturing site may be routinely sent to head office for reporting purposes. If duplicates are already produced, you should be able to arrange for these to be the vital records copies, and the only additional expense will then be storage. However, if duplicates need to be produced specially, this will obviously involve extra expense, and you will need to look for the most cost-effective solution, taking account of *all* the costs involved – facilities, equipment and staff time. You will also need to consider whether duplicates should be produced when the records are originally created or received, or subsequently, and therefore where this will be done and who will do it, taking account of scheduling and productivity issues.

There are two key points to bear in mind if you are considering duplication as a method of preserving vital records. First, a copy may not have the same legal value as the original and legal admissibility could be seriously compromised if records are copied to another medium without adequate controls over the conversion process. So make sure that you get professional advice. Secondly, at the risk of stating the obvious, the more copies there are of a record, the more records there are to manage. Duplication of any kind increases the time and expense involved in managing records.

Having decided how and when to duplicate vital records, you need to consider the storage options. Large organizations which have more than one operating site can store one site's records on another. Smaller organizations which only have one site will need to look at taking on additional premises or at commercial storage facilities. If the organization already has off-site storage facilities, this may be the obvious answer, provided that the facilities and systems are of the required standard.

Secure storage

There's no such thing as risk-free storage, only storage which minimizes specific risks. We will discuss storage equipment for active and inactive records in Chapters 6 and 7. Start with these chapters to identify the minimum requirements for storing any records, then increase the specification to get as close to eliminating the risk as possible. What you need will depend on:

> the volume of records to be protected
> whether the records concerned are active or inactive, and therefore whether they need to be stored close to working areas, or whether they can be stored off-site
> what risks the records will be exposed to while they are being stored.

For example:

> small quantities of active records which need to be stored close to working areas in an old building which is not constructed of fire-resistant materials, should be stored in a fire safe
> larger quantities should be stored in a fireproof vault which has automatic systems to detect and extinguish any fire which might break out inside it
> inactive records should be stored off-site in a detached, fire-resistant building with automatic systems for detecting and extinguishing fires.

Your actual storage will depend on the type of buildings available, how quickly records need to be retrieved, and, of course, the costs. In specifying facilities or equipment, make sure that you use established standards. There are national and international standards for the

65

construction of fireproof vaults. There are also established standards for safes, but remember that there's a critical difference between a safe which is designed to prevent unauthorized access to the contents and one which is designed to protect the contents from the effects of fire. Burglar-proof safes become ovens when they are exposed to intense heat. Storing records in them will mean that the records will be baked if there is a fire. Paper records may be salvageable. Records on microfilm, magnetic or optical media will be destroyed. So make sure that you choose the right equipment for the right purpose, and rely on the advice of independent research bodies and standards organizations such as Underwriters' Laboratories, rather than on the claims of equipment suppliers.

Don't forget . . .

. . . that if your vital records are in a technology-dependent medium, you need to make sure that the technology is preserved as well as the records. If you duplicate your computerized accounts to computer output microfilm, you'll need a microfilm reader to access the records. If you duplicate to CD, you'll need a CD drive. It's amazing how often these small details are overlooked in disaster planning.

Keeping it going

You can identify vital records and take measures to protect them, but this is only 'the end of the beginning'. Managing vital records to make sure that they are up to date and accessible is a 'vital activity'. Otherwise in the event of a disaster, the organization may find that they are useless. Managing vital records must become a part of the organization's normal work.

The first priority is to make sure that identification and protection of vital records is included in the organization's disaster prevention and business recovery plans. Whoever is responsible for these plans will be a key ally. If your organization doesn't have any disaster prevention or business recovery plans, you need to be careful how you raise the issue, unless of course you want to end up with wider responsibilities!

Responsibilities for identifying and protecting vital records must also be clearly defined. Procedures covering how and when vital records are to be updated or replaced must be clearly set out and communicated. Everyone involved must understand the importance of their role in maintaining vital records, so it will be essential to provide briefings and possibly training for them.

And finally . . .

. . . don't forget to organize procedures to access and retrieve vital records in an emergency. Make sure that you have lists and indexes which indicate what records there are and exactly where they are. Make sure that there are people on stand-by who are

> authorized to retrieve records, particularly security-classified material
> able to access the storage areas – do they have keys, or know where to get them?
> able to use any equipment which is required to retrieve the records – eg computers, microfilm equipment, pulpit ladders or forklift trucks.

Always prepare for the worst possible situation – remember that disasters usually happen in the middle of the night, on public holidays, in the middle of the winter, when there's a storm and there's been a power failure!

Summary

> **Vital records represent about 5% of all your organization's records.**
> **Without its vital records, your organization may not be able to stay in business after a disaster, so protecting them is an investment in the form of insurance.**
> **Learning from other organizations' mistakes is a lot less painful and expensive than learning from your own.**

Chapter 5
Survival tactics
Storage and retrieval

In this chapter you'll find out:

➢ **what records need to be protected from**
➢ **how to protect them.**

Now that you know what records your organization has, how they are used, how long they need to be kept and whether they are vital or not, you are ready to plan how to store them effectively, and retrieve them efficiently when they are needed. Your objectives are:

➢ to ensure that records can be retrieved easily within an acceptable time
➢ to prevent unauthorized access to them
➢ to protect them from physical deterioration or damage so that they survive for as long as they need to be kept.

Protecting records

The major risk factors for records are poor environmental conditions, natural disasters, accidents and crime. Let's look at these in a bit more detail.

Environmental conditions

Records will be damaged if they are stored in inappropriate environmental conditions. What is 'inappropriate' obviously depends on what the records are. Different storage media have different tolerances for exposure to heat and cold, humidity and dryness, direct sunlight and environmental pollution.

Natural disasters

Natural disasters can have catastrophic effects on buildings and on records stored in them. Floods caused by heavy rain, fires caused by lightning strikes and structural damage caused by high winds are among the most common in the UK, but the list goes on for other parts of the world: tornadoes, avalanches, bush fires, earthquakes, tidal waves . . . You need to assess the risks for your organization realistically, without going 'over the top'.

Accidents

Records can be damaged by fire, water, blast, impact, pressure or friction as a result of accidents. For example:

> ➤ plant or equipment failures, e.g. accidental discharging of sprinkler systems, breakdown of air conditioning systems
> ➤ power failures or surges
> ➤ collapsing buildings, floors, roofs, shelves.

And don't forget the human factor. People at work are usually busy, with too much to do, and too little time to do it. So sometimes they are impatient, clumsy and careless. They eat doughnuts over computer keyboards. They drink tea while they are reading documents (and put their mugs down on CDs!). They casually discard cigarette ends. They leave floppy disks on windowsills and laptop computers on trains. Of course, *we* never do anything like that . . . do we?

Crime

Your organization may be a target for criminals, either directly or indirectly. It may be located in an area which has a high crime rate, or which is a target for terrorists. For example, many organizations in the City of London took additional measures to protect records after they saw the devastation caused by the IRA bombs at the Baltic Exchange and in

Bishopsgate. Your organization may also be a target because of the nature of its business. Recent examples in the UK include attacks on companies involved in the development of genetically modified foods, and on others which undertake drug testing on animals.

Obviously, you'll need to work with other people in your organization to identify all the potential risks to its premises and records, and to determine the best way to manage them. You should do this *before* you make any decisions about storage facilities or equipment.

Not all records need to be stored in the same way. Vital records (see Chapter 4) need to be stored in first-class conditions, but these represent a very small proportion of the total volume of records held by an organization. Most records have a very short life, and their loss would not have a devastating effect on business operations. For these, 'standard class accommodation' is perfectly adequate. Even so, I can guess what you're thinking at this point: 'This is completely over the top. Management in this organization will never take this seriously.' If so, you need to remind them that records are the organization's most important information resource. By definition, they are irreplaceable or can be reconstituted only at very great cost. Point out that few organizations which have serious fires on their premises go out of business because they have lost all their furniture. Many do go out of business if they lose all their records. Unfortunately it's easier to get support and resources for managing records *after* a disaster than before one, but it's still important to try to do it the right way round.

What can you do?

First, avoid storing records in obviously high-risk locations. A location may be high-risk because of its geography or because of activities carried out nearby. For instance, it may be close to a river or standing water, which increases the risks of flooding, dampness and rodents. It may be next to a chemical factory or a heavy industrial area where there are significant risks of explosions, fires and pollution. It may be at the end of an airport runway or next to a major road junction, where accidents could have a devastating impact, in all senses of the word. It may be at the bottom of a mountain or a slag heap, where a landslide or rock fall could result in unintentional permanent preservation of the contents. It's just common sense, but you'd be surprised where some organizations do store their records.

Secondly, follow the established standards for the storage and handling of records. There are British and international standards for the storage and handling of paper documents, magnetic and optical media, film and various other materials. You need to be familiar with the ones which are relevant to the records in your organization. If there are no directly applicable standards, you'll need to work with the staff responsible for the records to assess the risks and determine the best way to store them. Look at what other organizations with similar records do, and follow accepted best practice.

Thirdly, make sure that people who use records understand how to do so properly, particularly if equipment is involved (for example don't leave files hanging out of cabinets, put CDs in their boxes). And last but not least, develop contingency plans for risks which you can't avoid.

Preventing unauthorized access to records

Storing records securely extends beyond ensuring that they are protected from physical harm. It also involves preventing unauthorized access to them. This can mean:

> preventing access to *information about records*
> preventing access to the *records themselves*
> in the case of electronic records, preventing access to, and manipulation of, the *data content of records*.

Access to information about records

Most organizations keep information about their records to themselves, for the obvious reason that it can be very revealing about their business and affairs. For example, file lists and electronic directory structures can contain the names of clients or customers – this would be very valuable information for competitors. Some also want to keep information about records confidential internally, only allowing staff to see information about records which they have to deal with in the course of their work. This is the ultimate in 'need to know' culture.

Access to records

All organizations want to prevent outsiders from gaining access to their records for obvious reasons: to protect their commercial and other business interests; to protect their intellectual property; to protect their legal rights, and those of others. Most organizations also have records which are restricted to certain individuals or groups of staff, either because they contain key commercial, technical or management information, or because they contain information relating to individuals which needs to be protected by law, for example, under data protection legislation.

Access to content

Legal admissibility is a key concern with electronic records. Establishing the legal admissibility of a document is about proving that it is authentic and genuine, ie that it has not been tampered with. Preventing unauthorized access to editable versions of electronic documents is therefore vitally important.

When you are assessing the security requirements of any particular group of records, make sure that you distinguish between these three categories. Be clear what it is you're trying to prevent unauthorized access to. Then consider who might want – or unintentionally get – it.

Visitors

Most organizations have security procedures which require visitors to be constantly accompanied by a member of staff. This doesn't always happen. Visitors get left in offices while their hosts get coffee, take phone calls or make photocopies. They are directed to toilets rather than taken there. It's usually assumed that visitors are trustworthy, but of course not all of them are. Records which are left on desks or in open filing cabinets are obviously vulnerable to casual – or purposeful – nosing about, and computer screens can be read from further away than you might think.

Contractors

Contractors are also usually assumed to be trustworthy, and, again, not all of them are. If you want to find out what's going on in an organization, one of the fastest ways is to get a temporary job with one of their contract service companies. If you go into an office wearing a uniform and carrying a bucket and squeegee/light bulb/screwdriver, it's fairly unlikely that anyone will challenge you. Again, records which are on open view are vulnerable. Amazingly enough, people also often assume that contract cleaning or maintenance staff are unintelligent or unobservant. Not so!

Passers-by

I've actually seen someone walking along a busy street stop and bend down to read a document which had fallen down between a desk and the full-length window of an office facing onto the street! I hope it wasn't your office. I've also watched someone rummaging through rubbish awaiting collection at a well-known company, apparently because there was some reasonable quality stationery visible in the boxes. I wasn't particularly surprised to see that the files he picked up weren't empty.

Others up to no good

Depending on the nature of your organization's business, you may need to consider the possibilities of reporters posing as window cleaners, private investigators posing as reporters and extremists posing as anything. Your organization must be extra vigilant if it is involved with high-profile individuals or 'hot' topics.

Obviously you can't be responsible for general security issues single-handedly. You have to:

➤ work with those responsible for managing premises and security to deal with specific issues, such as supervision of visitors
➤ persuade those with the budgets to provide enough storage space so that there's somewhere for records to go when they're not being used

> make everyone aware of the risks of leaving records on open view.

Employees

Of course staff need access to records to do their work. But do they need access to anything and everything? Is there any reason why they shouldn't have access to anything and everything? You need to work with the management in each area to determine how confidential individual records are, and how secure they need to be. It might be necessary to have secure filing cabinets. On the other hand, if your organization has electronic security systems, as an increasing number do, it may be possible to simply restrict access to particular areas of the premises, removing the need for such expensive filing equipment. If access to records does need to be restricted, you need to make sure that security measures are applied consistently. This may mean working with the IT department on security measures for electronic records, and with other specialists for records which aren't documents.

Of course it's important to identify all the potential security risks to your organization's records, but it's also important to assess them realistically because security is expensive and can get in the way of efficiency and productivity. So are industrial spies a realistic risk or do you just need to keep out casual Nosey Parkers? Should you spend thousands on window blinds, or just get people to tidy up? A low-budget campaign to increase staff awareness may be more effective than a large capital budget for safes.

Retrieval

There's no point in storing records unless they can be retrieved within an acceptable timescale. As a general rule, what is acceptable depends on whether the records are active or inactive. As a rough guide, active records are those which are used at least once a month. People need to be able to access active records quickly, whereas inactive records are usually needed less urgently. Figure 5.1 provides a summary of generally acceptable retrieval times.

The difference in the acceptable retrieval times for hard copy and electronic records reflects the different expectations of average users.

	ACTIVE	INACTIVE
Hard copy records	Fast access is essential – 20 minutes maximum.	Retrieval on the next working day is usually acceptable, with provision for emergency retrieval.
Electronic records	Very fast access is essential – one minute maximum.	Access within two–three hours is usually acceptable.

Fig. 5.1 *Acceptable retrieval times*

People expect computers to be fast and paper to be slow. According to recent studies, the average computer user is only prepared to wait for one minute for an electronic document to appear on the screen before calling the IT department to complain. This same user is prepared to wait for 20 minutes for a paper file to be delivered, and regards this as good service.

As a general rule, active records should be stored on the site where they are used, and inactive records should be stored off-site.

Exercise

Look at the records in your own working area – on your desk, in filing cabinets and cupboards, on shelves. Make a list of the main groups of records, estimate the volume of each group, and add it up. Mark each group as active or inactive. Split them up if you need to, for example putting this year's invoices under active and last year's under inactive. What proportion of the records are inactive? If the honest answer is 'None', award yourself a large whatever-you-fancy immediately. If it's more than a quarter of the total volume, you need to ask yourself why they're there and plan some time to sort them out.

Ask a colleague in other area to do the same. How do your results compare?

Does this happen all over the organization? If so, what needs to be done?

Chapters 6 and 7 deal with the storage and retrieval issues for active and inactive records in detail. This is where the challenge really starts because you'll almost certainly be under pressure to keep costs down and you'll probably also have to deal with:

> the generally low profile of the topic – it's hard to get people's interest in storage and security unless you get it wrong
> the fact that even people who aren't interested want to give you the benefit of their opinions – have you ever met anybody who didn't have an opinion on which filing cabinets work best, even if they make . . .
> . . . assumptions about information technology – 'We shouldn't need all this paper' or 'We won't need all this for long, we're going to scan it all'?

Summary

> **Good storage conditions are important - remember that records are the organization's most important information resource.**
> **The major risks to records are poor environmental conditions, natural disasters, accidents and crime. And, of course, people!**
> **You need to protect records against unauthorised access, but does this mean protecting information about records, the physical items themselves, or their data content? Or all three?**
> **There's no point in storing records unless they can be retrieved as and when they are needed.**

Chapter 6
Essential, everywhere, EXPENSIVE!
Managing active records

> **In this chapter you'll find out:**
>
> ➤ **how to decide where to store active records**
> ➤ **how to choose storage equipment and supplies for active records**
> ➤ **how to control active records.**

Active records are used frequently, so they must be easily and quickly accessible. This means that they must be stored relatively close to where they are used, which of course usually means in office space – the most expensive space in any organization.

The cost of space

Not surprisingly, the most expensive office space in the UK is in London. The rental cost can be as much as £500* per square metre, per year for the most prestigious accommodation. By contrast, some of the cheapest office space is in Swansea, where the rental cost of high-quality space is around £50* per square metre, per year. One square metre is approximately 10.5 square feet. So at these prices, a square foot could cost nearly £50 in London and nearly £5 in Swansea. One square foot is enough for a wastebasket. A four-drawer filing cabinet needs 9 square feet, costing £450 in London or £45 in Swansea. A 6-foot lateral filing cabinet needs 12 square feet, costing £600 in London or £60 in Swansea. *Every year*.

* April 1999 prices

Because it is expensive, office space is usually at a premium and everything has to justify its place there. Storing records – even active records – is not generally seen as a productive use of this space. In any case, offices are not ideal places for records. The environmental conditions are usually unsuitable for long-term storage, and where there are lots of people and lots of equipment, there are lots of hazards.

So as well as your overall objectives for storage and retrieval, which we looked at in Chapter 5, you have these specific objectives for active records:

> ➤ to provide enough storage space . . .
> ➤ . . . in the minimum amount of expensive floor space
> ➤ to move records out of office space as soon as possible.

So where exactly should active records be stored?

There's 'office space' and 'office space'. Active records must be accessible within 20 minutes, but this doesn't mean that they all need to be within arm's length, whatever the users may say. Distance is not the issue, and 'out of sight' shouldn't mean 'out of mind'. To determine where any particular group of records should be stored, you need to ask three key questions:

1 How many people use these records?
2 How often?
3 When they need them, how quickly do they need them?

Number of users?

If only one person ever uses the records, it makes sense to store them near to that person. On the other hand, if they are shared by a large number of users, they should be stored somewhere that is equally convenient – or inconvenient – for everyone.

Frequency of use?

If the records are in *constant* use, they should be stored as close as possible to the people who use them. Otherwise people will take files out of storage and pile them up anywhere that's more convenient – on their desks, on the floor . . . then no-one else can find them, and they are more likely to be lost or damaged. Records which are used less often can usually be stored a bit further away, but ask the next question before you finally decide.

Speed of retrieval?

You can usually divide active records into at least two categories:

A records which do need to be literally at arm's length – 'I need to be able to put my hand on this immediately, within 30 seconds to a minute';

B records which can be a bit further away – 'I need to be able to get my hands on this within 15-20 minutes'.

The 'arm's length' records should be as close as possible to the people who use them. How far away the others can be depends on the type of premises you occupy. But remember that you can go a long way in 20 minutes. An average healthy adult can walk a mile.

The answers to these three questions will tell you where the records *should ideally* be stored. Where they *can actually* be stored may be a different matter. You'll need to work with your organization's space-planners to identify potential storage locations that meet your requirements – space, location, environmental conditions and security. And you'll almost certainly have to compromise.

Most organizations have at least two possible places to store active records: at the desk and 'somewhere else'. Let's look at two examples to illustrate this, using the time-based categories defined above.

> **Management consulting firm, media group**
> The practice occupies levels 1-4 in a shared office complex. The media group occupies the whole of level 2. It shares a central set of client files with the rest of the practice. Although these files are in constant use, they are designated as category B records. Each project team has its own set of project files, which are category A.
>
> Category A: within one minute in shared cabinets next to the team workstations
> Category B: within 15–20 minutes in central files on the third floor

> **Charity, fundraising department**
> The organization occupies all of a four-storey building. The fundraising team is split between the first and third floors.
>
> Category A: next to workstation
> Category B: in central files on the third floor

Some organizations have more than two possible places for storing such active records. If yours does, remember that too many locations can confuse and irritate users without providing any real benefit. However, a few don't even have two possible locations. Pressure on space may mean that there's no room for 'at the desk' storage, or alternatively, that there can only be 'at the desk' storage. On the other hand, some organizations have adopted working patterns which make 'at the desk' storage impractical or inefficient – for example, hot-desking, shift-working – so that centralized filing is the only option.

Whatever the options are, when the storage space has been allocated and you know how much floor space you've got to work with, you need to select suitable storage equipment. At this point you should remember that most offices have not been designed to store large quantities of records.

Selecting storage equipment

When you're selecting storage equipment, define your requirements first and consider *all* the options – don't rule anything out too soon.

Define your requirements first

To define your requirements, think about what you need the equipment to *do*:

> ➢ provide enough storage space within the allocated floor space
> ➢ protect the records from physical damage
> ➢ prevent unauthorized access to the records
> ➢ enable quick and easy access and retrieval.

Space

What types of records need to be stored – paper files? microfiche? videos? CD-ROMs? How many of each, approximately? From this you can calculate the total amount of storage space required, normally measured in linear feet/metres, and then work out the storage density that you need. You should allow some room for growth in your calculations, because, as a rule, new records come in faster than inactive or redundant ones go out.

Protection

What are the specific risks in the storage environment? Consider these in the context of the general risks in the premises to determine whether any special features are needed, such as environmentally controlled cabinets.

Security

Do the records need to be secure? How secure? Consider this in the context of the general security of the premises to determine whether special security features are needed.

Retrieval

How many people will need access to the records? How many at the same time? If lots of people are using the records at the same time, the equipment needs to be easy to get to, quick and simple to use, and robust enough to take the strain.

Now you have a functional specification for storage equipment. Here are two examples to illustrate the point.

Architect's practice

The material to be stored is project files and related materials for current projects. These consist of hard copy files, loose photographs, videotapes, models, design boards and samples of materials such as bricks, glass, tiles, carpets, paints, fabrics. The total volume is approximately 500 linear feet.

The space available is a room of approximately 400 square feet with a ceiling height of 8 feet. There are no obstructions. The room is located off the main work area on the ground floor of the building and is fitted with smoke detectors and sprinklers.

The records are vital to the business and highly confidential but as visitors to the building are always accompanied by staff, the priority is protecting the records in the event of a fire or similar disaster.

The room will be used by both secretaries and architects daily, with the busiest periods mid-morning and at the end of the day.

Management consultancy firm

The material to be stored is client files and project files. These are central hard copy files for the whole practice. They are A4 files.

The space available is on the third floor of a 1988 office complex. It is an area of approximately 400 square feet with a ceiling height of 8 feet, located in the middle of the open-plan office. The whole office is fitted with smoke detectors and sprinklers.

The files are in constant use by consultants and administrative staff for filing and retrieval. The files are confidential to the practice and given the fact that the building is shared with other companies, the files need to be secured against unauthorized access out of office hours as well as protected in the event of a fire.

Don't forget . . .

At this point you need to identify any constraints on what you can do with the available space. Are there any obstructions, for example, pillars? Are there any other restrictions on the use of the floor, for example, access to under-floor ducting or power points? What's the ceiling height, and are there any obstructions, for example, suspended lighting or ducting? What's the floor-loading capacity? Can any of these constraints be removed by structural or other work, and how much has to be accepted as 'given'?

Consider all the options

There are lots of different kinds of equipment for storing active records. The most common are:

➢ filing cabinets
➢ vertical cabinets, with drawers
➢ lateral cabinets, with shelves plus other fitments – hanging rails for suspension files, pull-out frames for drop filing, trays and racks for microfiche and computer disks and tapes, etc.
➢ open shelving
➢ circular rotating carousel units
➢ revolving double-sided units
➢ mobile shelving
➢ mechanized vertical carousel systems.

A detailed description of these different types of equipment is given in Chapter 5 of *How to Manage Your Records* (see Further Reading on page 175), and magazines like *Office Equipment News* are good sources of information about existing and new products if you don't want to approach suppliers directly. What we're focusing on here is how you determine which of these, or which combination, of them, will best meet your needs. In assessing the suitability of any piece of equipment, the key questions to ask are:

➢ will it make efficient use of space?

> ➤ will it protect the records from physical deterioration or damage?
> ➤ will it provide appropriate security?
> ➤ will it be safe and easy to use?
> ➤ what will it cost?

Will it make efficient use of space?

Some types of storage equipment are more space-efficient than others. The measure for this is called the storage density ratio and you calculate it like this:

> ➤ *divide* the storage capacity of the equipment
> ➤ *by* the amount of floor space which it requires: 'footprint' + access space.

This tells you how much you can store in one square foot / metre of floor space. The higher the ratio, the more space efficient the equipment is. Here are some examples.

Table 6.1 *Ratio of storage capacity to floor space*

Equipment	Floor space (square feet)	Storage (linear feet)	Storage density ratio
4-drawer vertical filing cabinet	9	8	1 : 0.9
7-foot, 6-shelf lateral filing cabinet	12	18	1 : 1.5
5-tier rotary carousel unit	17	30	1 : 1.8

But remember your constraints, particularly floor-loading. The higher the storage density, the greater the weight. Yours wouldn't be the first mobile shelving installation to fall through the floor.

Will it protect the records from physical deterioration or damage?

You'll need to rely on information from independent research organizations, your own personal experience and the experiences of current users ,to assess how well any piece of equipment will survive a fire, flood, explosion or other disaster, and how well it will protect the records from damage if it does survive. Here are a few pointers.

1 Most storage equipment is not made to withstand explosions or being dropped.

2 Metal and other fire-resistant materials are obviously preferable to flammable materials.

3 Some equipment will only protect the contents if it's used properly. Doors and shutters only work if they are closed. Pull-down shutters tend to be left open, simply because it's a pain (literally, if you have a bad back) to keep opening and closing them. Be realistic about what users are likely to do.

4 Introducing electrical power introduces additional risks. Electrically powered mobile shelving or carousel units are more vulnerable to fires caused by electrical faults.

5 Think about how particular types of equipment will be affected by existing fire detection and extinguishing systems. For example, a gas fire suppression system will not function properly in a room filled with mobile shelving because the gas will not be able to penetrate between closed aisles. Records stored on equipment which is open at the top will be especially vulnerable to water damage from sprinkler systems.

6 Water damage can come from above or below. To minimize damage to records in a flood, it's good practice to store them at least six inches off the floor.

Will it provide appropriate security?

Remember that really determined criminals will get access to whatever they want access to, and that the biggest risks in most organizations are carelessness and casual inquisitiveness.

> **Think about it . . .**
> How many people in your office have you seen doing any of these things?
>
> ➤ leaving filing cabinets unlocked or open
> ➤ sharing or writing down computer passwords and keypad codes
> ➤ sharing swipe cards
> ➤ leaving computers switched on while desks are unattended
> ➤ leaving files open on desks or other places where they can be read
> ➤ taking records out of the office to meetings or to work on at home
> ➤ holding security doors open for people, particularly visitors and contractors.

Most storage equipment can be secured against everyone but the most determined criminal. There are simple locks and combination locks and electronic locks. There are security bars and double-skinned cabinets and alarms. Obviously, the more security features you want, and the more sophisticated they are, the more you'll have to pay. Be realistic about what's needed and what will actually be used. Don't pay for security features you don't need or you know won't be used. A simple campaign of training and awareness can be more effective in improving the overall security of records in the organization than filing cabinets with electronic locks operated by swipe cards, particularly if you can tie it in to other general security awareness measures. Remember that removing temptation is half the battle. Marking a document TOP SECRET is the easiest way to draw attention to it.

Will it be safe and easy to use?

It's reasonable to assume that storage equipment which is manufactured to appropriate British or international standards will be safe to use. In other words, it won't actually injure people who use it, *provided that they use it properly*. These are some of the issues you need to think about.

1 Will users need basic health and safety training, for example, to show them how to lift things correctly? The Manual Handling

Regulations 1993 require all staff who have to lift and move things as part of their work to be trained to do so safely.

2 Will people need to be trained to use the equipment? With any kind of powered equipment, the answer is definitely 'Yes', but they may also need to be shown how to fill vertical filing cabinets so that they don't tip over, and how to use lateral cabinets so that they don't get knocked unconscious by a rapidly descending pull-down shutter.

3 Will additional equipment be needed? For example, will steps be needed to reach high shelves?

4 Will an average person find the equipment easy to use? Is a particular level of strength or mobility required? Will bending and stretching be necessary? For example, manually-operated mobile shelving can be tricky to get moving.

When you're thinking about how efficient equipment will be to use, think first about the likely patterns of use. Some equipment is easy to use if only one person wants to use it at a time, but very inefficient if several people show up at once. Vertical filing cabinets are a good example. It doesn't matter which drawer you're looking in, somebody else always wants a different one! Similar problems can occur with mobile shelving, vertical carousels and rotary carousels. So think about how many people will use the records, how many at the same time, and what kind of problems could arise.

Don't forget to consider how the equipment works, and how 'independent' it is. Electrically operated equipment won't work without power. If someone pinches all the step-stools, you won't be able to reach high shelves.

Just a word about aesthetics . . .

Storage for active records does need to harmonize with the working environment. Even if it's in a closed room, people are still going to be using it every day. Appearance shouldn't drive your decisions one way or the other – much of the filing equipment in modern offices was chosen by architects and office designers and is completely unsuitable – but you do need to remember the importance of making records look and feel part of the working environment.

What will it cost?

Don't let the purchase price of the equipment drive the decision-making process. Make sure that you look at the big picture. Think about:

1 What will it cost to buy?
2 What other costs will be involved? Depending on what you choose, you may need structural work, electrical work, carpentry or painting and decorating. If the equipment requires bespoke filing supplies which are only supplied by the manufacturer of the equipment, they probably won't be cheap (and it's a disaster if the manufacturer goes out of business).
3 How long will it last?
4 What will it cost to maintain? All mechanized equipment needs regular servicing and maintenance.
5 Will it be reliable, and if not, what will it cost to fix? What can go wrong? Think about jammed doors, lost combinations, broken keys, breakdowns . . .
6 Will it be fast and efficient to use? Time is money. Can several people access records at the same time, or only one person – and does this matter?

Of course, if you do have a limited budget and you can't afford the equipment you want, or enough of it, remember that there's more than one way to crack a nut. Do you *really* need to store all these records here? Should some of them be destroyed? Are they *really* active? Can more of them be sent to inactive storage (see Chapter 7)? Have you considered alternative ways of keeping them: microfilming, scanning or only having the electronic versions immediately to hand?

Take your time over selecting equipment. Whatever you choose must be efficient, effective, economical and appropriate. It may be expensive, and it will probably be around for a long time. You'll have plenty of time to regret a bad choice, and you'll never hear the end of it from the users – or the management, if it starts to cost a lot to maintain or repair.

Selecting filing supplies

There are hundreds of different kinds of folders, suspension files, storage boxes, indexing tabs, labels and other paraphernalia designed to make filing and retrieval more efficient. When you're looking at them, think about:

> ➤ the records
> ➤ the storage equipment
> ➤ the users
> ➤ quality
> ➤ costs.

The records

The whole point of folders, files and boxes is to contain the records. Here are a few other things to bear in mind:

> ➤ containers should fit the records – not too big, not too small. For example, foolscap-size paper doesn't fit in A4-size folders or files.
> ➤ keep laser-printed and photocopied paper documents away from plastic wallets or binders – it doesn't take long for them to stick together, and the print comes off the paper when they are separated.
> ➤ don't file papers which have long retention periods in folders with steel fastenings – they rust.

The storage equipment

With apologies to Mr Micawber,

> ➤ foolscap drawers, foolscap files – no problem, but do you really need them these days?
> ➤ foolscap drawers, A4 files – a waste of space
> ➤ A4 drawers, A4 files – perfect
> ➤ A4 drawers, foolscap files – AARGH!

Things which overhang the edges of shelves get damaged by the shelves cutting into them and by people going past. If they are in filing cabinets, they get damaged by the doors closing – if they will close at all, that is. In an ideal world you'd start with the records, choose the filing supplies and then choose the equipment. Of course this isn't an ideal world so you just need to keep reminding yourself of the basics.

The users

What are the files – or whatever – like to use? Simple? Fiddly? Frustrating? Think about the people who will be doing the filing. They will be handling whatever you select all day, every day. You need to make their jobs faster and easier, not more complicated. Think about the people who will be using the files. You need to make it easy for them to get what they want quickly. Always get samples of the things you are considering using – most manufacturers or stationery companies provide free samples – and ask some of the people who'll actually be using them to try them out. And listen to what they say, because they'll remember what they told you.

Quality

Lightweight folders are fine for records which have a short life and don't get used very much. But if records are active for a long time and are handled a lot, then the folders and boxes they are stored in need to be much more robust. Again, always get samples and test them before you buy large quantities. Remember that price is not a reliable indicator of quality, and don't rely on the manufacturer's claims and pretty pictures in catalogues. It's better to find out that Cheep-O suspension files don't stay suspended if you put anything in them *before* you order five thousand of them.

Cost

If what you need costs more than you would like it to, shop around. Remember that holding stock is a waste of money and space – filing supplies are rarely needed that urgently – so only do this if you get a really good price. Again, look at the big picture:

> ➤ buying cheap supplies which don't last the course, and then buying more to replace them, is false economy
> ➤ keep it simple and avoid gimmicks
> ➤ think about recycling, as in 'using again' – when you destroy records or send them to long-term storage, you can take them out of the folders and boxes and use these again.

And remember that if records are worth keeping, it's important to look after them properly.

Controlling active records

You know the story. You need a file. You know it should be in the filing system. You go to the filing cabinet. Is it there? No. You follow your nose for half an hour, asking everyone around if they've seen it/got it, and then one of several things usually happens:

1 You find it at the bottom of a pile on someone else's desk. This gives you the opportunity to shout/moan/nag and feel superior before you get back to work.
2 You give up and go back to your desk, where you find the file at the bottom of one of your piles. You settle down to your work quietly and hope no-one's noticed (trying to think up some credible responses to 'So where was it then?').
3 You redo the work/grovel to the customer/make excuses as required, and then blame everyone else and criticize the filing system.

There are very few things more time-wasting and stressful than searching for records. People must be able to find them quickly and easily. If they are not available for any reason, this must be immediately obvious. So you need to have good finding aids and an effective tracking system. Finding aids tell people where records should be, i.e. their normal storage location. Tracking systems tell them where they are when they're 'out'.

As an information professional, you'll already be familiar with the idea of finding aids – things which help people to find records. You'll also know that they can be handwritten lists, typed card indexes or computer databases, but that what really matters is that they are up to date and well organized, and contain sufficient detail to allow users to identify and locate relevant records quickly.

The most popular methods of tracking active records are:

> OUT registers – bound or loose-leaf registers in which the users write the details of records which they remove from the storage system
> OUT cards or folders, on which users write their name and which take the place of removed records
> computerized tracking systems.

You can buy OUT registers and cards as standard stationery items or have them custom-made. You can make your own by drawing columns in a notebook or drawing up a form in a word processing package and printing it on card. Figure 6.1 is an example of a simple OUT card which is intended to replace the file on the shelf when it's removed. Computerized tracking systems work like this:

> details of each record are entered into a computer database and each item is given a barcode
> details of each user are entered into the database and each user is given a barcode
> every time the record moves, the user scans the barcode on the file and his/her own barcode
> the database is instantly updated with the new location details.

They combine finding aids and tracking in a single system, and speed up the process of removing and returning records. And of course technology is always sexier than a book with a biro on a string! They are certainly worth looking at if you have money to spend.

In the end, it doesn't matter whether the tracking system is simple or sophisticated, cheap or expensive. The main thing is that there is one.

FILE REFERENCE	A – 2 – B	
DATE	**OUT TO**	
	NAME	**SIGNATURE**

Fig. 6.1 *An OUT card*

However, whether any tracking system works effectively depends *entirely* on the users following two simple rules:

1 If you take something away, record the fact.
2 When you've finished with it, put it back in the right place.

If you work in a library, you know what's coming next. *Whatever* the system is, most people will use it most of the time and some people will never use it because they are always too busy or because they think it's too petty and bureaucratic. There's not much you can do about them and it's not worth losing sleep over. You can only put good systems in place and monitor how well they work.

Summary

➤ Active records need to be stored near to where they are used, so that they can be retrieved quickly and easily.

➤ Decide where and how they need to be stored before you choose storage equipment.

➤ Choose your equipment and supplies carefully – look at the big picture and avoid being cost-driven.

Chapter 7
Undervalued, under-resourced – under the building?
Managing inactive records

In this chapter you'll find out:

➤ how to decide where to store non-current records
➤ how to choose storage facilities, equipment and supplies
➤ how to control inactive records.

Inactive records, by definition, are not retrieved frequently, and when they are, speed is not usually very important. This means that they can, and should, be stored away from the workplace, because keeping records which are not frequently used in high-value and expensive office space simply cannot be justified. In any case, offices are risky places for records, so moving them out as soon as they don't actually have to be there is a good idea. However, some records have very long retention periods, and can be inactive for many years. Storing them for a long time, even in much cheaper space, can be costly. Also, because they are not immediately to hand, retrieving them can be inconvenient and expensive. So you need to manage them effectively. Which means that, as well as your overall objectives for storage and retrieval (see Chapter 5), you have these specific objectives for inactive records:

➤ to provide enough storage space for them, for as long as they need to be retained
➤ to minimize storage and retrieval costs
➤ to make sure that they are disposed of promptly when their retention periods expire.

The challenge is to achieve the optimum balance between cost and convenience to meet routine requirements, and still be able to deal with the exceptions, like needing to retrieve records urgently.

So where exactly should inactive records be stored?

Well, there's the basement . . .

If your organization has premises with basement accommodation this may seem like the obvious solution. If you've got space on the premises, why even consider other options? Here's why.

Basements are not suitable places for storing records

Basements are high-risk areas. First, to state the obvious, they are underground. Underground facilities may be more resilient to missile attacks, but they are much more vulnerable to the more common risks of flooding, dampness and pests. Secondly, plant and equipment – heating pipes, air conditioning ducts, electrical cabling, drains – tend to be located in basements. This greatly increases the risk of fire, flood and explosion. Thirdly, activities which are incompatible with office accommodation are often located in basements – things like maintenance services, waste disposal facilities, general storage, computer rooms, high-volume photocopying facilities. These activities also increase the risk of fire. Remember, too, that floods, fires and other incidents are more difficult to deal with underground, so their impact may be greater. It's true that some of the world's most effective records storage facilities have been established underground in, for example, disused deep mines, underground tunnels and nuclear shelters. However, these have three key things in common. They were set up with full knowledge of the risks and were designed and equipped to cope with the dangers. They are dedicated to the storage of records. The people who manage them are not dependent on others to control the risks. You are unlikely to be able to achieve this in the basement of the average office building.

Most basements and store rooms were not designed for storing large quantities of anything

Many were not 'designed' at all – they are simply 'spare space', and the amount which is usable is often limited because of ducting, cabling, pipes, drains and so on. If you have large quantities of records, it can be complicated and expensive to fit out such spaces, and difficult to justify compared to the other options.

Storing records may not be the most productive use of basements

With premises costs and pressure on office space increasing all the time, many organizations are being more creative about space planning. They are converting areas which are not suitable for offices into meeting rooms, training suites and computer facilities. Storage is, quite rightly, low on the priority list.

Storing records on-site may keep them in a high-risk environment

Your organization's main premises may be in a high-risk location in terms of environmental threats, crime or natural disasters (see Chapter 5). While active records have to be stored there, inactive records don't and it makes sense to remove as many records as possible to a lower-risk location so that they will survive if the worst should happen. Most organizations could reconstitute a significant proportion of their business from their inactive records if they had to. So, if you have any choice at all, keeping records on site should be the last resort.

So what about off-site?

To identify potentially suitable locations for off-site storage, you need to ask two key questions. How often are records likely to be retrieved and how quickly will they be needed?

Frequency of retrieval?

If records are likely to be retrieved frequently, they should be stored relatively close to the organization's working premises, otherwise retrieval costs may offset the savings in storage costs.

Speed of retrieval?

Retrieval on the following working day is usually acceptable for inactive records, so in theory they could be stored at a considerable distance from the main premises. However, it must be possible to retrieve records urgently. Depending on the nature of your business, this could mean anything from half an hour to half a day. As a rule, it's unlikely to be less than two hours. So think about it this way: in a well-organized storage facility, it should take no more than 15 minutes to locate and retrieve a record. How far can you get from your premises in an hour and a half? Don't be too ambitious – reliability is important especially to users whose records are going off-site for the first time. So if the storage facility is an hour and a half away by road, and someone needs the record in two hours, and its raining hard and it's the rush hour and there's been an accident on the road causing a massive traffic jam ... Be realistic when you're thinking about time and distance. It only takes one dissatisfied customer to undermine everyone's confidence in the arrangements.

Balancing the answers to these two questions will give you a geographical area to work within. What you can do in that area may be a different matter. However, it may be possible to use technology to overcome distance. For example, individual documents could be retrieved by staff at the storage facility and faxed to the requester, or information could be provided over the telephone if security procedures allow this.

Selecting storage facilities

As with selecting storage equipment for active records, define your requirements first and consider all the options – don't rule anything out too soon.

Define your requirements first

As with active records, the facilities need to:

➢ provide enough storage space
➢ protect the records from physical deterioration or damage

> ➤ prevent unauthorized access to the records
> ➤ enable access and retrieval within an acceptable timescale.

Space

There must be enough storage space to meet current needs and provide some room for growth. However efficiently the space is managed, it's unlikely that the volume of records going into storage will ever be exactly balanced by the volume going out to be destroyed or transferred to archives.

Current needs

What types of records are to be stored – paper files? microfiche? videos? CD-ROMs? How many of each (estimate!)? Are the records to be stored loose or in containers of some kind? If they are in containers, what kind and what size? With this information, you can calculate the total amount of storage space required, normally measured in linear feet/metres or cubic feet.

Growth

Planning for growth is always a bit of a shot in the dark. If you already have records in storage, you can start by predicting on the basis of past growth. For example, if the number of storage boxes has increased by 15% in each of the last five years, it's reasonable to assume that future growth will be at least this much. Then you need to take account of other factors which are likely to influence the rate of growth, such as the introduction of electronic systems or microfilming programmes. If you have nothing to go on, you'll just have to take an educated guess. In any event, take as much space as you can get because you don't want to have to move if you can avoid it.

Protection

Storage facilities must be designed to minimize or eliminate the risks to records which we discussed in Chapter 5. This outline of requirements should be regarded as a *minimum* standard.

Location

The site must not be in a high-risk location, for example, near to a water course or standing water, a motorway junction, a railway line, an airport runway or a heavy industrial site. It must be within 5 km or 5 minutes' travelling time of the nearest police and fire stations, and it must be accessible by more than one route so that emergencies can be dealt with promptly and so that services can be maintained if there are problems on one access route.

Construction

The building must be sound and constructed from fireproof materials. It must be leak-free and have effective drainage systems to prevent a build-up of water which might lead to flooding. All internal water pipes should be lagged and routed to minimize the danger from burst pipes. The floor must be strong enough to cope with the weight of the records, their containers and the racking or equipment in which they will be housed. It must be level to maintain the stability of equipment and it should be dustproof or at least sealed to prevent dust from being generated by abrasion of the floor.

Environmental conditions

There must be a ventilation system which prevents airborne pollution from entering the facility. An automatic fire detection system must be installed throughout the building. Ideally, there should also be an automatic fire suppression system, but bear in mind that standard sprinkler systems may cause more damage than a fire. The environmental conditions in the storage area must be stable, maintaining temperature and relative humidity levels within the recommended ranges for the media being stored.

Use

Records storage should be the only activity undertaken in the building. Storing other materials in the same building greatly increases the risk of fire breaking out or taking hold. If there are other activities on the same site, they must not involve storage or handling of high-risk materials such as hazardous chemicals, petroleum products or timber.

Physical security

All points of access to the site must be secure. The storage facility itself must be in a detached building and must not share space with other operations on the site. All points of access to the facility must be secure. External doors must have access controls and fire doors should be permanently alarmed. If there are windows they must be protected with bars or grilles. The records themselves should be stored in containers as a basic deterrent to casual nosiness or vandalism.

Management

Smoking must not be permitted *anywhere* on the site. Management must ensure that this policy is rigorously enforced, with disciplinary sanctions for their staff and penalties for contractors. The site must be kept clean and free from accumulations of rubbish.

Prevention of unauthorized access

Removing records from office areas removes temptation from casual Nosey Parkers, but secluded storage facilities can be a target for more determined snoopers. Physical security measures are obviously important in preventing unauthorized access to records, but these must be supplemented by effective management controls. Access to the storage and work areas must be restricted to staff whose main job is to store and retrieve records, and they must be trained to understand the need for tight security. Only authorized individuals should be allowed to request retrieval of records, and all requests should be checked. As far as the records themselves are concerned, anonymity is the best (and cheapest) security. Records containers should only be marked with codes which link them to the lists of their contents. In particular, they must not be marked with anything which identifies the organization, the originating department or the contents. Any finding aids which are held in the storage facility must be secure. Hard copy documents must be kept in locked cabinets when they are not in use, and computer systems must be pass-word-protected. Finally, frequent unplanned security inspections must be carried out to ensure that security equipment and systems are in good condition and that security procedures are being followed.

Now you have a functional specification for storage accommodation.

Consider all the options

The basic choices are to set up an in-house facility, or to use a commercial records storage company. Setting up an in-house facility means that your organization takes on suitable premises, equips them to the appropriate standards, takes on staff to manage and run the facility and establishes systems to enable staff to store and retrieve records. Commercial records storage companies provide storage and retrieval services from their own premises. All of them will collect and deliver records from and to your premises. Most of them can supply storage boxes and other containers. Some offer additional services such as cataloguing and destruction. The companies in the market fall into three broad categories:

1 Companies which specialize in records storage and retrieval, i.e. storage and handling of records is their *sole* business.
2 Companies which have substantial records storage and retrieval operations, but which also have other business activities – usually things which have an *apparent* synergy – such as removals and general storage.
3 General storage companies, which will store and retrieve anything.

The range and quality of their facilities and services varies enormously. Costs, however, tend to be fairly consistent when you compare 'like with like'. In deciding whether to 'buy or DIY', the key issues you need to consider are security (in the widest sense), service provision and cost.

Security

In an in-house facility, you control what is stored there. In a commercial facility, the company controls what is stored. You have to rely on them not to store anything which might pose a risk to your records. In an in-house facility, you control the quality of the premises and the storage environment. You can upgrade or economize as you feel appropriate or necessary, taking account of any risks which may be involved. In a commercial facility, the company determines the quality of the facilities. If it decides to upgrade or economize, you have to accept it or terminate your contract.

If your organization's records are stored in-house, there is virtually no risk of them being disclosed unintentionally by staff to a third-party. If they are stored in a commercial storage facility, there are two risks which you need to be aware of. First, storage companies often show potential customers around. Unless your records are completely 'anonymous', these people will know that you use that facility. Does this matter? Secondly, the company may accidentally deliver your records to another customer. Even with the best will in the world, it does happen. People make mistakes.

In an in-house facility, you control the quality and performance of the staff who handle your records. In a commercial facility, the company controls the staff and you have to rely on it to ensure that its staff are 'legal, decent, honest and truthful' and that they are properly trained to do their jobs.

Service provision

In an in-house facility, you are in control of the services which are provided. You can agree on retrieval arrangements with the users of the records, and provide these if you have sufficient resources. You can determine the arrangements for transferring new records to storage. If you use a commercial storage company, you can only have the services and service levels which they provide. If your requirements change, they may not be able to meet them, and again you may have no choice but to terminate the contract.

Cost

You need to look at the big picture. For an in-house facility, think about:

> ➤ premises – capital (purchase) or revenue (rental) costs
> ➤ storage and handling equipment – ditto

> ➤ computer systems and equipment – if they have to be purchased specially
> ➤ staff – fully built-up costs
> ➤ supplies – containers, stationery etc
> ➤ transport costs – vehicles, couriers etc.

For a commercial facility, think about:

> ➤ storage charges
> ➤ service charges – initial take-on of new material, retrieval, transport, delivery
> ➤ exit costs – what the company will charge you to release your records if you terminate the contract.

The big difference is obviously that if you set up your own facility, you have to take on all the set-up and running costs, and pay them whether the facility is empty or full. If you use a commercial company you 'pay as you go' for storage and services, and none of the other costs are your concern. If the storage facility is full, it's their problem. If you destroy records, you stop paying for the space they occupied – filling empty space is also their problem. Another difference is handling growth. If you outgrow your own facility, you have to make other arrangements. If demand for services increases, you may have to take on more staff or buy more vehicles to cope. If you use a commercial storage company, they will usually be able to provide you with extra space as you need it, and to scale up their services to meet increased demand. Of course the company will want to increase its prices from time to time, but you will probably be able to negotiate a contract price for a fixed period.

There's no right or wrong answer. It's vital to define your requirements first, and know where you can compromise. For a start, what you need may not be available commercially, in which case you'll have no choice but to 'do-it-yourself'. If a commercial storage company can provide what you want, then you must produce a full cost-benefit case which takes account of both your immediate and your long-term needs, making sure that you compare like with like. In the end, the key issue is how much control you want or need. Using a commercial company always means compromising on control.

If you decide to 'buy', you must define your requirements for facilities and services comprehensively and precisely *before* you talk to any potential vendors. Once you know exactly what you need, identify potential suppliers, invite tenders or proposals, and evaluate them very carefully. This process is time-consuming and requires specialist knowledge and skills, so make use of any professional procurement expertise in your organization, or engage a consultant who has experience in this area. Once you have a contract in place, you must actively manage the supplier relationship. It's vital to keep in touch with what's going on and to make sure that standards are maintained. You should get what you're paying for on the last day of the contract as well as the first.

Controlling inactive records

Wherever your records are stored, they need to be controlled. Like active records, they need to be organized logically and indexed so that they can be found again when they are needed. They need to be tracked so that you know what's where at any given time. And, most importantly, they need to be promptly destroyed or transferred to archives at the appropriate time.

Organization and indexing

There's more to storing records than dropping them into a cardboard box, writing 'John's files' on the outside of the box and sending them off to 'archives'. There's no point in keeping records unless they can be retrieved, so it's essential to record what is sent to storage. The best way to do this is to use a standard form, usually called a Records Transmittal List or a Records Transfer List (see Figure 7.1). These can be filled in by hand or produced by setting up a template in a word-processing application, or a report format in a computer database. Whatever the format, there must be more than one copy of the list. One must be kept by the user, to refer to when something needs to be retrieved. One should go in the box, so that if it should go astray, whoever finds it will be able to identify the contents and the 'owner' (this, of course, emphasizes how

RECORDS TRANSFER LIST				
Use one list for each box				
DIVISION		**BOX NUMBER**	10035	
DEPARTMENT		**COST CENTRE CODE**		
TRANSFER DATE		**DESTRUCTION DATE**		
Reference	Description / Title		Dates	
			From	To

Fig. 7.1 *Records Transfer List*

important it is not to let boxes go astray). One might also go with the box, to be kept by the people who manage the storage facility, although this may not be wise if the boxes are stored with a commercial storage company.

Retrieval

Inactive records are generally easier to track than active records. Because access to storage facilities is restricted, retrieval requests are channelled through a single point where they can be recorded. The same applies to retrieved items which are being returned to storage. Remember, though, that when records are returned to their owners, they get lost or mislaid just as easily as active records.

Retention

Inactive records should have defined retention periods, or at least defined times at which they will be reviewed to determine their ongoing value. It's important to make sure that whatever is meant to happen does happen, and at the right time. In Chapter 3, we discussed the risks of retaining records which should have been destroyed. In addition, even in dedicated storage areas, space is not infinitely expandable, so it's important to move redundant material out to make room for records which do need to be kept. What you need is a variation on a tracking or bring-forward system which tells you what to do and when. This can be done manually, using card indexes or forms, or on a computer system. Just as long as it's done.

Summary

➤ **Inactive records can be stored away from the workplace because they are not retrieved so often and, when they are, time is not usually that important.**
➤ **Off-site is better than on-site.**
➤ **Buy or DIY – but do it properly.**

Chapter 8
It's just a load of rubbish!
Destroying records when you no longer need them

In this chapter you'll learn:

➢ why it's important to destroy records properly
➢ how you can destroy records
➢ the key issues to consider.

Recent cases reported in the press have illustrated the importance of destroying records resonsibly. For example,

➢ adoption files were dumped by a local council and found by members of the public when they were blown off a landfill site
➢ PCs were dumped by a council social services department. A local man bought one of them from the dump for £10 and discovered that it contained social services files on child abuse cases.
➢ drafts of classified reports containing information about planned redundancies were thrown in the wastebin by a secretary in a blue-chip company. They were leaked by the manual workers who handled the company's waste and who were among those to be made redundant.

These cases caused embarrassment and sometimes financial loss to the organizations responsible, and, more importantly, considerable distress to the individuals who could be identified from the records.

It's a fair bet that for every such incident reported in the press, there are a dozen more. Disposal of records is often the weak link in the records management chain because most organizations just don't see any risk. Managers say things like, 'But it's just a load of rubbish. Who would be interested in it?' Good question. They should give some serious thought to answering it, and these days they should also be asking themselves, 'Who else could be damaged or embarrassed by disclosure of these records?' Records which have no further value to the organization might still contain information which could:

> be very valuable to competitors
> damage the organization's reputation or commercial interests, if it was inappropriately disclosed
> damage the interests or reputations of other organizations or people. Your organization could then be liable for damages for breach of confidentiality.

So you need to make sure that if your organization doesn't want its records any more, they are disposed of in the right way. There must be no risk of sensitive information falling into the wrong hands.

Disposal or destruction?

There's a crucial difference between disposing of something and destroying it. Disposing of something simply means throwing it out. In most office environments, this means putting records in wastebaskets under desks and next to photocopiers. This 'rubbish' is then dealt with as office waste, normally through a public waste disposal system involving landfill sites. Don't even think of this as a way to destroy records which contain sensitive information. It's much quicker to send them straight to *The Independent* yourself and cut out the middle man! Only non-sensitive and public domain material should be disposed of in the normal office waste system. Everything else should be destroyed, which means 'obliterated'.

Everything?

Yes, everything. Even the surplus printouts and the extra unwanted copies. Even the horrible smudged printouts and the half-copied documents from the jammed photocopier. Even the handwritten notes for a report or presentation. Everything. I realize that this might sound a bit over the top, but there really are people who spend their time rummaging through skips and waste sacks, hoping to find commercially sensitive or politically damaging information. In the US, they call them 'dumpster divers'. Here we call them 'security advisers' or 'private investigators'. And they are more common than you might think. So are disaffected employees looking to cause trouble. But even if these risks seem very small, all organizations have records which they wouldn't want outsiders to see, whether they are drafts or final versions, and whether they were produced yesterday or 20 years ago. So what should you do?

Choosing a destruction method

There are several ways to destroy records. In deciding which method is the most appropriate for your organization, your first priority must be security. Then you need to think about costs and environmental impact.

Security

How 'destroyed' do the records need to be? If the biggest risk is nosy office cleaners, simple shredding may be all that's necessary. On the other hand, if

> your organization could be a target for industrial or political espionage
> the records contain sensitive or personal information

you'll need to make sure that they can't be recovered and reconstituted.

Costs

The costs of destruction depend on

> how simple or sophisticated the destruction process itself is
> how much preparation and handling is involved, such as removing documents from containers
> whether you do it in-house or through a specialist contractor.

As with retention and storage, don't let cost drive the decision-making process. Some methods of destruction are relatively more expensive than others but, as always, look at the big picture and compare the costs of doing it in-house and buying specialist services.

Environmental impact

If your organization has an environmental policy which states its views on the use of chemicals, environmental pollution and similar issues, make sure that you take account of this when you are deciding how records should be destroyed, and how the resulting waste should be disposed of. Obviously it would be embarrassing for Greenpeace to be found dumping its unwanted records at sea, or for the National Trust to be discovered dumping waste on its heritage sites.

Destruction methods

Shredding

There are two kinds of shredding: *strip shredding* produces 'spaghetti' and *cross-cut shredding* produces 'confetti'. Shredding is most commonly used for paper documents, but there are machines available which can shred plastics such as microfilm, acetate presentation slides and plastic wallets, and there's even one that can shred CDs.

Security

Size definitely matters! The smaller the pieces, the less likely it is that the document could be reassembled by someone with enough patience and sticky tape. I know this seems unlikely, but it really does happen. Remember those Iranian students who overran the US embassy in Tehran in 1979? They seized shredded waste and reconstructed many classified documents. Closer to home, there have been several reported cases of highly classified commercial documents being fished out of rubbish skips by rivals. Don't private investigators have exciting lives! So cross-cut shredding is always more secure than strip shredding. If this is a big concern for your organization, there is a German standard which specifies sizes for shredded pieces for different levels of security classification. For secret documents, it specifies pieces not larger than 2mm by 15mm. For even more highly classified documents, pieces should be not larger than 0.8mm by 13mm. Even the most dedicated jigsaw puzzle freak would give up with that.

Costs

Shredders are now regarded as standard office equipment. They come in various sizes for a range of situations : wastebasket-size which fit under desks, photocopier-size for standard office use, and very large with hoppers for large-scale destruction. Price depends on size and sophistication. Strip shredders are cheaper than cross-cut shredders, size for size. As a rule of thumb, the smaller the pieces you want, the higher the cost of the equipment.

One issue which is often overlooked is that preparing documents for shredding can be very time-consuming – removing containers and folders which can't be shredded, taking out staples and paper clips, and so on – and time is money.

Environmental impact

Dumping shredded waste in landfill sites isn't environmentally friendly, particularly as it's much more bulky than the original documents. You may be able to recover some of your costs by selling it as waste paper for recycling.

Grinding

Grinding reduces almost anything to very small particles.

Security

The particles are impossible to reassemble, so this is a very secure way of destroying records. This is why it's used by armed services, government departments and embassies.

Costs

Equipment ranges from so-called 'office' models to industrial-size machines, and cost obviously varies accordingly. The great advantage of this method is that no preparation is required.

Environmental impact

Again, dumping the waste in landfill sites isn't environmentally friendly, but you may be able to recover some of your costs by selling paper waste for recycling.

Degaussing

Degaussing means demagnetizing magnetic media, such as computer tapes and disks, and video and audio tapes. It literally wipes them clean, and they can then be re-used.

Security

Degaussing is generally a very effective way of removing data, and it's certainly more secure than simply reformatting disks. However, there's always a risk that data could still be recovered from computer tapes and disks, given enough time, money and patience, so physical destruction is still the best option for highly classified records.

Costs

Degaussers come in a range of sizes, from hand-held models to large units, and again costs vary according to size. They tend to be used in large-scale computer environments. If your organization already uses this method of dealing with magnetic media, it could be very cost-effective.

Environmental impact

Magnetic media which have been degaussed can be re-used, so this is a nice green option.

A combination of destruction methods may be the answer, depending on the security classification of the records concerned. Here's an example.

Table 8.1 *Destruction methods related to security classification*

	Unclassified	Restricted	Confidential
Paper	Strip shredding	Cross-cut shredding	Pulping, maceration or incineration
Magnetic media	Reformatting	Degaussing	Maceration

Controlling records which are due for destruction

Physical security

Records need to be kept secure until they are actually destroyed. So don't leave them unattended in corridors, reception areas or loading bays.

Authorization

Destruction of records should be authorized by a manager who is responsible for the records and able to commit the organization to any consequences of destroying them. Of course, this is where it can all go wrong. Managers are busy and if you send them lists of records which are due for destruction, asking them to review them and sign to authorize destruction, what reaction are you most likely to get? Exactly – piles of records all over the place waiting to be signed-off. On the other hand, if your records retention policy states that records will be destroyed automatically when their retention periods expire unless you have been officially informed that destruction should be delayed, there will be no risk of over-retention, and no piles of records lying around. However, you may risk destroying something which has become relevant because of a change in circumstances.

Documentation

It's important to keep a record of which records have been destroyed, and when. Even if records are destroyed 'automatically' at the end of their retention periods, you should keep a record of the fact that it was done, to show that the documents were destroyed in the normal course of business, and in a properly authorized way.

DIY or buy?

If your organization generates large quantities of records and takes security seriously, you'll need to weigh up the pros and cons of handling destruction in-house or buying specialist services. If you can afford them, specialist companies take a lot of the hassle out of destroying records securely. They will provide bags and bins for collecting material to be destroyed. They will come and take the stuff away. They will store it, prepare it if necessary and destroy it. They will pass it to a recycling company if you want this. They will provide destruction certificates. Some will even let you go and 'supervise' the destruction of your records, although rumour has it that this is even more boring than filing!

Summary

➤ If records are no longer relevant, make sure that they are securely destroyed.
➤ Choose an appropriate destruction method, thinking about security, cost and environmental issues.
➤ Consider using specialist contractors – they take a lot of hassle out of the physical process of destruction.
➤ Keep a record of what is destroyed.

Chapter 9
It's not a record – is it?
Managing e-mail

In this chapter you'll learn:

➢ that e-mail messages can be records
➢ what to do with them if they are.

Lots of articles about 'managing e-mail' have appeared in newspapers and journals over the last couple of years. They have looked at e-mail from many different perspectives: improved productivity, corporate security, personal privacy and knowledge management to name a few. However, here, we're only interested in e-mail from a records management point of view. And your first question may be . . .

Are e-mail messages records?

Well, they *might* be. It depends. Let's recap. Records are *documents or other items* containing recorded information, which are produced or received *as part of a business activity*. Well, e-mail messages are certainly documents. And at least some of the e-mail messages in your organization must be produced or received in the course of business! So they will be records. It's really as simple as that. So . . .

If e-mail messages are records, what should you do with them?

The same as you should do with all other records:

➢ organize and index them

> store them and put a system in place so that they can be retrieved
> retain them so long as they are needed, and then destroy them.

These issues are all discussed in other chapters. The key issue that we need to address here is this: e-mail messages can be records, but e-mail systems are not record-keeping systems. E-mail systems are person-to-person communications systems. They are designed to store messages for individuals, or groups of individuals. They are the electronic equivalent of the 'IN', 'PENDING' and 'FILE' trays. So when you identify an e-mail message as a record, and you want to keep it as a record, you must put it into a record-keeping system.

Your first challenge will be communicating this to the people in your organization! You are likely to encounter at least some 'mine, mine, mine!' reactions. E-mail looks and feels personal. This was one of the things that 'sold' it as a technology in the first place. However, many organizations are now discovering that the way their employees use and abuse e-mail is creating significant risks for them. They are attempting to claw back control by establishing e-mail policies setting out what employees can and can't use e-mail for, and how they may and may not use it. Unfortunately, these policies still tend not to consider the risks of using e-mail systems as record-keeping systems. Which is where you come in.

You need to ensure that your organization's records management policy explicitly covers e-mail messages, and that its e-mail policy includes specific guidance on what to do with e-mail messages which are corporate records.

What are the options ?

Again, it depends. If your organization's record-keeping systems are completely paper-based, the only option is to print e-mail messages and file them in paper files. On the other hand, if there are formal electronic filing systems, like the ones we discussed in Chapter 2, you should file e-mail messages into them. Figure 9.1 shows a folder containing e-mail messages. Filing messages in these standard folders involves the 'Save As...' function in Windows, selecting 'Message

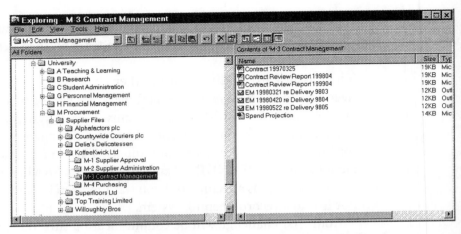

Fig. 9.1 *Folder containing e-mail messages (Windows Explorer)*

Format' as the Type, and naming the document according to the standard naming conventions.

Once e-mail messages are filed in record-keeping systems, whether electronic or paper, the same principles apply to them as to all other records, and you manage them in exactly the same way.

A final word of caution

If you identify an e-mail message as a record, you can transfer it to a record-keeping system and delete the copy in the e-mail system, or you can retain a copy of it in your mailbox so that you can do 'communication' things with it – forward it, reply to it and so on. If you retain copies remember that these are still records – they're just records which haven't been 'filed' in the 'official' system. They're the equivalent of the personal copies of things which people keep around their desks and offices. And as with paper 'personal filing systems', the records management challenge is to make sure that these systems are also managed, so that retention periods are applied consistently – if a particular record is supposed to be retained for two years and then destroyed, no copy of it should be retained for more than two years. In some organizations, e-mail systems are managed by the IT department. They backup and archive the systems regularly. In terms of retention, they tend to:

> either provide 'personal' allocations of space, pressing users to clear out their mailboxes when they are taking up too much space
> or clear out on a regular basis, eg all messages are destroyed after 90 days or six months.

In both cases, retention is driven by volume and space, which is contrary to what you're trying to achieve. The only solution is to include records management issues in e-mail policies and train users to understand what they need to do, why it's important and, most importantly, how to do it. You should then monitor whether they *do* do it, and take whatever action is appropriate with the support of senior management.

Managers in all sorts of organizations are becoming increasingly aware of the risks of e-mail, as well as its benefits, so this is a good time to get to grips with the records management headaches it can cause.

Summary

> **E-mail messages can be records, but . . .**
> **. . . e-mail systems are not record-keeping systems, so . . .**
> **. . . e-mail messages which are records need to be taken out of the e-mail application and put into a formal electronic or paper filing system, and then managed like all other records.**

Chapter 10
Will the last person to leave please switch off the light!
Managing records through organizational upheaval

In this chapter you'll find out:

➤ **what can happen to records during organizational upheavals**
➤ **how to cope with the most common corporate adventures.**

Change is a constant factor in organizations. Mergers and demergers, reorganization and restructuring, upsizing and downsizing, relocations and closures have become part of normal working life. Managing records effectively through such upheavals is vitally important to protect the interests of the organization and its stakeholders, but it can often seem like an impossible task. Let's look at some of the most common situations and some strategies for dealing with them.

Relocation

Organizations generally relocate to new premises for more space, less space or cheaper space, but very few move to accommodation which has more space for storing records. So the most common records management issue in the run-up to a relocation is reducing the volume of active records which need to be stored in offices. The problem is that this is usually seen not as a *records* management issue, but as a *facilities* management issue, and not as a 'corporate' task, but as a 'personal' task. Staff are usually told to 'have a clear-out' but what they clear out, and how, is left up to them. If you've ever been involved in an office move, you know what happens next. Very few people get organized in advance. Instead of reviewing 'their files' in good time to decide what they need to take with them, and what can be sent to storage or destroyed, they leave everything to the last minute. On the day before the move, records to be taken to the new office get flung into crates (usually too many!), records to be sent to storage get dropped into boxes ('Sorry – no time to list them') and everything else gets shoved into bins or left behind for the new tenant or the bulldozer to deal with. After the move, people find that records are missing, and it's anybody's guess where they might be. If questions are ever asked, they say 'Well, we lost it in the move. You know what moves are like', and everyone rolls their eyes and agrees.

This is disastrous from a records management point of view. If people clear out 'their files' or the records in 'their offices' under pressure of time and entirely on their own judgment, it's highly likely that some important records will be destroyed and that a lot of junk will be kept. If they don't take care over how records are packed or moved, things will get lost. If they don't make sure that 'their junk' is destroyed properly, records may fall into the wrong hands. The potential consequences for the organization – loss of knowledge, financial penalties, public embarrassment – are very serious. This is no way to deal with the organization's most important information resource.

So what should you do?

A relocation is a major event, usually set up as a project with a project manager and a project team, consisting of people who deal with all of the major issues concerned with closing down one office, fitting out another and moving into it. Try to get onto the project team. This is the best way to make sure that records issues have a high enough profile in the run-up to the relocation. If you can't get onto the team, you must liaise closely with the project manager to make sure that he understands the records management issues and how they should be dealt with. You also need to make sure that he knows that you can help with planning storage for records and controlling the actual removal.

Space planning

First, you need to make sure that staff are *not* told to have a clear-out. In fact they must be told *not* to have a clear out. Next, you need the facts:

> the amount of records currently being stored, ie what's in filing cabinets, in cupboards and on shelves, *plus* all the piles, boxes and other stuff lying around
> the storage capacity of the space available for records in the new office
> the required reduction, ie subtract storage capacity from amount of records.

This information may be available from the relocation project manager. If not, you'll need to find out for yourself. Do a brief survey to find out the amount of records currently being stored, and examine floor plans and furniture specifications for the new office to calculate storage capacity. Then you can think about how to achieve this reduction. These are the basic options:

1 Reduce the volume of records to be stored by :
   – destroying redundant records
   – storing inactive records somewhere other than in office space
   – making records physically smaller by converting them to, say, microfilm or digital media.
2 Increase the space available for storage by:
   – allocating more floor space in the new office
   – increasing the volume capacity of the same space by using higher density storage equipment.

The 'right' answer will probably be a combination of these, depending on the reduction required, the timescale for the relocation and the budgets available. The decision trees in Figures 10.1 and 10.2 show the logical approach to the records management issues involved. The same principles apply whether you're dealing with a hundred files or hundreds of thousands, and whether you need to reduce the volume by 15% or 70%. Work logically through the issues and decide what to do in a balanced way – and be realistic about what you can do in the time available with the resources you have. Almost everything takes more time and money than you think it will, and if anything can go wrong, it will. So this is not the best time to decide to go out on the 'leading edge'. While

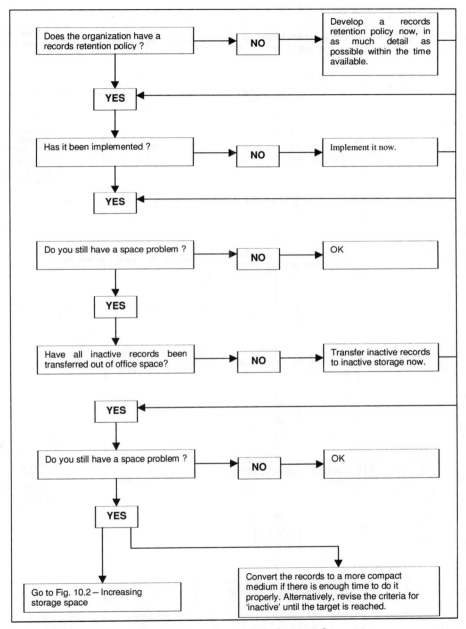

Fig. 10.1 *Reducing the volume of records to be stored*

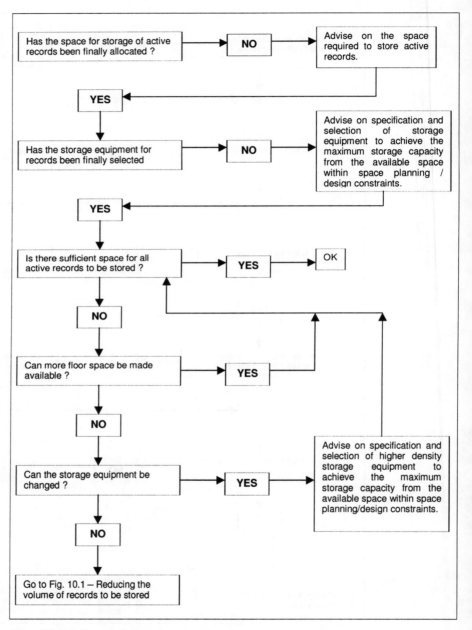

Fig. 10.2 *Increasing storage space*

a document management system may look like just what you need for those files, so that you won't have to throw any of them away (!), deciding to scan a million documents six months before you relocate, when you've never scanned anything before, would be, as they say in the Civil Service, 'a courageous decision, Minister'. Similarly, this is probably not the time to introduce a new colour-coded filing system which will require every member of staff to go on a one-day training course to learn how to use it. It would be better to save these initiatives for after the move, when everything has settled down. When you've made the decision, plan, plan and plan again. Here are some things to think about.

1   Make sure that everything has a planned destination, either a space in the new office, or a place in storage. Don't rely on it being 'all right on the night'. If you know that there won't be room for something in the new office, don't plan to send it there and hope for the best. Throw it away or send it to storage – you can always get it back later if it turns out that space is available.

2   Make sure that records will fit into the space allocated to them. For example, if files are being put into new filing cabinets, will they actually fit?

3   Make sure that any additional equipment will be immediately available. For example, if records are being converted to microfilm, are there microfilm readers already or do they need to be bought? If new filing cabinets mean that staff will need step-stools to reach the top shelves, do these need to be bought?

4   Make sure that records are in a fit state to be moved. For example, if file covers are so tatty that they're falling off, they might need to be changed to prevent documents being damaged during the removal.

Above all, focus on what must get done in advance so that records which are really needed for active work can be stored efficiently and used effectively in the new office. Don't get side-tracked into dealing with things which are not 'mission critical'. These things can be changed after the move, if they really need to be.

Finally, it's worth saying that, even if you're relocating to bigger premises and are in the very fortunate position of not having to reduce the volume of records held in office space, you should still review the records that are held to identify redundant and inactive material and deal with it appropriately. It makes no sense at all to spend time and money moving records which you don't need, even if there is space for them in the new office. The relocation manager will certainly appreciate anything which streamlines the move, saves money and stops people from filling the nice new office with junk. And, quite simply, you shouldn't miss any opportunity to improve records management practices in your organization.

Moving

Moving offices is essentially the same as moving house. The only real difference is scale. So if you've ever moved house, you know what you need to do to move records from one location to another: count them all out at one end and count them all in at the other end. The objectives are to make sure that everything gets moved and to minimize downtime. So this means

> ➤ packing records carefully so that everything will be in the right order for unpacking, and so that nothing will be damaged en route
> ➤ making a record of what's in each container, so that if anything is needed urgently, it can be easily found
> ➤ labelling containers accurately so that they go to the right place in the new office, and in the right order for unpacking
> ➤ checking that all the containers have arrived and are in the right place before unpacking anything.

If the advance planning was done well, there should be no crates stacked up with nowhere to put the contents.

Internal restructuring

Organizations restructure for many reasons, but the scenarios are predictable. New departments may be set up, existing departments may be merged or split up, and functions or activities may be reallocated to other departments. The records management issues here are obvious. New departments need new records systems to be set up to support their work. The records of departments which are split or merged, or which have their functions and activities reallocated, need to be reorganized to match.

So what should you do?

Setting up

The creation of a new department is in many ways the easiest situation to deal with. If the organization already has records management policies in place, all you have to do is set up new systems for the new areas in compliance with these policies. If there are no policies in place, you can set up new standalone systems from first principles. What you need to set up initially will obviously depend on the nature of the organization and the immediate operational priorities. Filing systems and storage for active records are usually the top priorities. However, you should obviously plan to cover all of the core issues in the medium to long-term, by developing a records retention policy, identifying and protecting vital records, and making appropriate provision for storage of inactive records so that they can be routinely transferred out of office space. The managers of new departments are often prepared to be innovative, so there may be opportunities to try out new ideas and approaches, as 'pilots' or 'trials' for future developments. This may be the time to reach for that new document management system or colour-coded filing system, while you can try it on a small scale.

Merging or splitting

The creation of 'new' departments by moving, splitting or merging existing departments, and the reallocation of functions and activities between departments is tricky because records need to be moved, split or merged to match. As far as filing systems are concerned, if all the systems involved are well designed (i.e. based on organizational functions and activities), and have been designed in the same way, it's relatively easy to move files out of one system and into another. The biggest headache may well be the amount of storage space available, which doesn't always increase proportionately to the size of the department. However, moving files between systems which have been designed in different ways is at best difficult and worst a nightmare. The only really effective solution to this problem is to design new filing systems for the areas concerned.

These new systems should operate from 'Day One', and only essential active documents should be transferred into them from the previous systems. The rest should be transferred to inactive storage for retention in accordance with the records retention policy or for later review. This may sound drastic, but converting files from one filing system to another which has been designed in a different way, involves at least reclassifying all files, sometimes even splitting files and reclassifying individual documents (in which case it might even be necessary to photocopy documents, to put a copy on each new file). All of this is extremely labour-intensive and time-consuming, and it's rarely necessary. Remember that 85% of all documents which are filed are never retrieved anyway. Provided that the documents and files from the previous systems are listed before they are transferred to inactive storage, they can be retrieved if they are ever needed. Of course, another way to deal with the physical aspects of merging or splitting active files would be to introduce an appropriate electronic document management system which could manage documents according to the new classification scheme. But whether you go for a high-tech or a low-tech approach, provided that the new filing system is well designed, future reorganizations will be much easier to deal with.

Merging or splitting inactive records is something which you should consider very carefully. It might just be change for the sake of change, and, again, it's labour-intensive and time-consuming. Don't do it unless you can see real benefits in terms of speed or ease of retrieval, or cost of storage. Always ask yourself, 'Would it really matter if we didn't?' Merging or splitting IT systems, such as records management databases, is also a matter of judgment and should be driven by the users concerned. If systems become difficult to use, they must be changed.

Mergers

Mergers invariably result in internal restructuring, so the same issues arise. However, anyone who has been involved in a merger will tell you that the restructuring is the easy bit – merging cultures is the real challenge. We've already discussed how an organization's culture influences its approach to managing its records. So the real challenge here is developing records management policies and systems which reflect the needs and culture of the new organization, rather than any one of the 'old' organizations. The other issue which you may need to consider following a merger is merging facilities and systems, such as inactive records centres and records management software.

So what should you do?

The principles and guidance given above on dealing with internal restructuring apply here, as far as handling active records is concerned, but bear in mind the cultural issues. Designing new systems may take longer and require more diplomatic effort on your part. When it comes to records management policies and procedures, simply merging what exists may not be feasible. For example, retention policies must be reassessed from the viewpoint of the new organization. The same applies to identifying vital records for disaster planning purposes. By all means work from what exists, but keep first principles in mind.

Merging physical facilities and IT systems takes time and costs money, so it's important to establish whether it's really necessary. Avoid change just for the sake of change now – it may make more sense to wait. Here are a couple of examples to illustrate this.

Two legal practices

Practice A, the smaller of the two, kept its active files in its general office, and its inactive files in the basement of its premises. The details were listed in a Dataease database.

Practice B also had its active records in the general office but its inactive records were stored with a third-party contractor. The details

(cont.)

Two legal practices (continued)
of all its records were listed in a Paradox database.

The practices offered complementary services to the same sectors and had many clients in common. They decided to merge.

Practice A moved out of its premises into vacant space in the building occupied by Practice B. Several new filing cabinets were purchased and all of the active files were integrated into one system. However, there was nowhere in the building to store inactive records, so Practice A's inactive files were sent for storage with the third-party contractor.

It was obvious that the databases needed to be merged, but both of the databases were several years old and did not really meet the needs of the legal staff for fast easy access to information about clients' files. Most importantly, neither was Windows-based. It was decided that the most appropriate solution was to wait until the practice upgraded its IT system to Windows 95 and to then transfer all the data into a new Microsoft Access database. It took a year to complete, and this time was used to update and 'clean up' the data in the old databases ready for uploading into the new Access database.

Two colleges
Collegea A andB merged. They each had their own 'archives' of inactive records. One had the details of its records recorded in a Microsoft Access database, the other used RECORDIT, an off-the-shelf records management software package. The merger involved some staff and students moving from one site to the other, but there was no need to move either of the 'archives' and no immediate need to merge the databases. When records needed to be sent to the archives, they were simply sent to the nearest store and were recorded on the relevant database. However, it soon became obvious that while the physical location of the material was irrelevant (records could be made available from either store within half a day), the fact that people had to know where something was before they could request it was inconvenient, so the data from the Access database was transferred to the records management application.

Closure

Whether it's a car manufacturer closing down an unprofitable plant, a company closing a regional sales office following a merger or an abolished quango transferring its responsibilities to a government department, all closure situations present the same risks to records. The dangers are that they will be lost, damaged or inappropriately destroyed in the heat of the moment by staff who don't know what to do with them, rather than controlled and kept securely for as long as they need to be retained by the organization itself or by its 'successors'.

Dealing with records in these situations is more complicated if staff are being made redundant. The announcement of redundancies has a predictable effect on morale, even among those who are not, or not immediately, affected. This means that standards are likely to fall, creating more problems than there would otherwise be. When staff actually leave, their knowledge of the business and its records goes with them. It is difficult for outsiders to identify records, to understand their purpose and to assess their ongoing value without access to this inside knowledge. It's particularly difficult if, when they go, they simply abandon records, leaving things where they lie on their last day at work. I spent the first year of my career as a records manager organizing the records left by the staff in various offices on a closed steelworks site. The wages office was the most amazing. It really was like the Marie Celeste. Everyone had stopped work at twelve o'clock on the last day – literally just dropped everything – and gone to the pub, and they never came back. So eighteen months later I found desks covered with papers, open files, piles on the floor, opened envelopes with the papers still inside – even half-drunk mugs of tea – all covered in dust, cobwebs and mould.

In fact, experience in large-scale closures shows that most people who are being made redundant are happy to cooperate in sorting out records in the run-down to closure, particularly if it keeps them in work for longer. Of course there are always the few who are not. These are the ones that take 'their files' home, steal confidential business plans to leak to the newspapers and plant 'time-bombs' in computer systems. This may be understandable as a human reaction, but it can cause great difficulties for an organization even in the final stages of its life.

131

So what should you do?

The reason for a closure tends to determine how it is managed, and how easy it is to deal with the organization's records as part of the process. Closure of a manufacturing site, for example, takes a long time and will normally be managed as a major project, with a project manager and a large project team. On the other hand, winding up a small company normally doesn't take very long and will only involve a few people. As with relocation projects, if there is a project team, try to get onto it to make sure that records issues are properly addressed in the run-down to closure. If you can't get onto the team, liaise closely with the project manager to make sure that he understands the records management issues and can provide the necessary direction and support to staff to do what they have to do. If it's a much less formal environment, liaise with whoever is making the major decisions and make sure that they understand what needs to be done with records before final closure.

Whether you're dealing with a factory employing 1,000 people or an office of 50, you need to follow the same plan of action.

1 Review the organization's active records to identify time-expired material which should be destroyed. If the organization already has a records retention policy, identifying time-expired material will be quick, easy and risk-free. If it doesn't, this isn't the time to develop one. The best approach is to remove any obvious junk (at 'container level' only, i.e. keeping or destroying whole files or storage boxes, not weeding through them) and set a review date for the rest. If the organization is continuing elsewhere, and you subsequently develop a retention policy for it, you can apply it retrospectively to these records. If the organization is closing down completely, those who are legally responsible for its affairs will also be responsible for seeing that its records are kept for the required period.

2 Destroy this time-expired material securely (see Chapter 8).

3 Transfer the remaining records to inactive storage (see Chapter 7). Obviously, if the site had its own store for inactive records, these will need to be transferred elsewhere, perhaps to one of the organi-

zation's other sites, or, if the whole organization is closing down, to a third-party storage facility.

Of course, the larger the establishment, the longer this process will all take, and the more time you have, the better. Make use of whatever inside knowledge is available to help with reviewing the records. Sometimes it's even possible to bring staff who have been made redundant back into the organization on short-term contracts to help with sorting out the records.

Summary

➤ **Whatever the crisis, focus on what's mission-critical and don't get sidetracked.**
➤ **Don't change for the sake of change. If change is constant, you'll be changing it all again soon anyway.**

Part 3
Managing your organization's records

Introduction

Now that you know what records are, why it's important to manage them and the general principles of good records management, you are ready to get to grips with managing your own organization's records. You will need to:

- ➤ define the goals
- ➤ find out what the current position is, and identify the gap between this and the goals
- ➤ decide how to close the gap
- ➤ do it.

The goals must be realistic, specific and measurable. 'Improve the way we manage our records' is not a good goal. Nor is 'Get rid of all this paper!'. Here are some 'good' examples:

> **Management consultancy practice, regional office**
> Goal: Improve the management of project files so that files are always up to date and can be located and retrieved by consultants within five minutes.

> **Architect's practice**
> Goal: Ensure that storage conditions for inactive records are compliant with relevant British and International standards.

You can't decide what the goals are. The goals are what 'the organization' wants to achieve by 'doing records management', which of course means what the managers want to achieve. If they don't know, why are you both-ering ? If they don't care, there's no point in doing anything. Of course, it may be that they simply haven't given any thought to it, and have no idea what records management could do for them, in which case you have some awareness-raising and marketing to do. You need to guide them to the point where they say, 'Great idea. We should do this because . . .' Then you know what the goals are and you can get on with it.

Part 3 takes you through the essentials of 'getting on with it':

> finding out about your organization and its records
> analysing this data to establish the current position and decide what to do next
> developing the framework of policies and procedures
> implementing them.

Chapter 11
What have you got to work with?
Finding out about your organization and its records

In this chapter you'll find out how to find out:

➤ **what your organization's business is, and what records it produces**
➤ **what makes your organization 'tick'**

so that you can plan how to manage its records.

If you get all the facts, your judgment can be right; if you don't get all the facts, it can't be right.   Bernard Baruch, US Presidential Advisor

Before you can plan how to manage your organization's records, you need to know what those records are. But that's only the start. You can't manage records in a vacuum. You have to manage them to meet your organization's specific business needs and in a way which fits your organization's unique style and culture. So now is the time for you to find out about *your* organization, its business and its records.

What you need to know

You need to start by getting an overview of the whole organization – what it does, how it does it and what records it generates. You also need to find out what makes the organization 'tick'. What *kind* of organization is it and how does it 'work'? The best way to do this is 'top-down' – starting with an arial view and then zooming in to look at individual divisions and departments, and how they link together. Whatever part of the organization you're looking at, these are the key questions you need to ask:

The organization

> What is the organizational structure? Is it 'flat' or is there a dizzying multi-level hierarchy?
> What is the organizational culture? Formal? Laid-back? Team-based or 'them and us'?
> What is the management style? Directive? Collaborative? How 'visible' are managers?
> How do things get done? Are people empowered to make their own decisions? Is everything done by committees or working parties? Is there a learning culture or a blame culture?
> How does the organization see itself, relative to others in its field? Innovative? Leading edge? Conservative (with a small 'c'!)? (If you're dealing with only one division or department, how does it see itself relative to the rest of the organization? The most important? The most efficient?)
> How do outsiders see the organization? Does it match how the organization sees itself?
> What is the staff profile, ie what are the relative numbers of professionals, technical staff, administrators, secretaries, clerical staff and manual workers? How does each group regard the others?

The business

> What are the core business functions and activities?
> What other functions and activities are carried out to support the core business? These usually include finance and accounts, personnel, facilities management, health and safety: What else?
> Are any of these functions and activities regulated by outside bodies such as auditors or regulatory authorities? Who/which? What does 'regulation' involve?

The records

> What records are produced or acquired by the organization? Why?
> – what are they for?
> Are they documents or 'other items'? If they are documents, what types? If they are not documents, what are they?
> How are they used? How often? By whom? Why?
> How are they currently managed? Even if there are no formal systems or procedures, the staff who hold and use records will be doing things with them. So how are records organized? Where and how are they stored? How long are they kept, and why? How are they disposed of when they are no longer needed? If any services are provided, such as off-site storage, who is providing them and how?
> Does the way they are currently managed meet the needs of the business? The basic business need is to have the right record in the right place at the right time. Is this happening? If not, why not? Are the services which are currently provided the right services and are they provided in the right way?

Finding out

If you've been with the organization for a while, you may know the answers to some of these questions already. It's a good idea to start by writing down what you do know. This will help you to check your assumptions and 'gut feelings', and to identify the gaps in your knowledge. On the other hand, if you're new to the organization, you have the advantages of a 'clean sheet' and the freedom to ask 'stupid' questions – the ones you don't want to ask if you've been around for a while because you think asking will make you look dim.

There are three tried and tested ways to get the information you need: reading things, talking to people and looking at the records, or, to put it in more technical terms, doing desk research, interviewing staff and carrying out records surveys. These are complementary tools and you really need to do all three to get the full picture of what *really* goes on in the organization, how things *really* get done and how records are *really* handled and used, as opposed to what people will tell you. To manage records effectively, you need to get beyond the politics, the gossip and the patch-protecting.

Desk Research

(If you're an information professional, you may want to skip this section.)

If the organization has a World Wide Web site and an intranet, start with these, but don't forget to check how up to date the information is. Otherwise start with the formal sources of information about the organization and its business, for example: annual reports and other official publications; press releases and similar PR materials; marketing materials; internal communication media such as magazines, videos, circulars etc.; the words of senior executives in the form of presentations, speeches, media interviews etc. Use your contacts to get hold of other useful materials, such as organization charts, strategic plans and management reports.

Interviewing staff

The most difficult thing about interviewing is deciding who you should talk to. If you interview the 'wrong' people, you'll waste their time and yours. You may also annoy or antagonize them, which is the last thing you need at this stage. So it's worth taking the time to identify the 'right' people. Start by defining very clearly – write it down! – what you want to know. Then find the people who have, or are likely to have, this information. If you're new to the organization, get your boss or other contacts to help you with this. Focus on what people do rather than where they fit in the organization. Knowledge and experience of the business areas and activities that you want to find out about counts for more than seniority (or lack of it). As a general rule, go for the *least* senior person in the organization who can tell you what you want to know. This may be the Director of Finance or the Payroll Administrator, the Professor of Medicine or his secretary – it doesn't matter as long as you get full and accurate answers to your questions. Don't automatically start with senior people and work your way 'down', unless this is 'the way we do things around here'. For a start, senior managers are less likely to have time to talk to you formally – their diaries are normally full for the next three months. Secondly, while their views on how the organization's records should be managed are extremely important and should shape any policies and procedures which you develop, they are not likely to have detailed information about how records are handled on a day-to-day basis, even in their own offices. Most senior managers have secretaries, PAs or administrators who deal with these 'administrative' issues.

When you've decided who you want to interview, think about whether you want to interview people one-to-one or in groups. Both have their advantages and disadvantages. One-to-one interviews are usually the best option if you have the time, but they can grind to a halt if the person being interviewed needs information from someone else. Group interviews are more 'efficient' time-wise but they can be difficult to control if you get a few people with strong views and a couple of red herrings. Don't get too hooked on planning, though. I've learned that however you would prefer to approach it, the interviewees' diaries usually decide. When you set up the appointments, make sure that you tell the people concerned what you want to discuss, so that they have time to prepare (whether they do prepare or not is a different matter!).

Interviewing is not as easy as Jeremy Paxman makes it look. Interviewing people in your own organization can be particularly daunting because there's a fair chance that you'll have to work with them again. If you haven't done much interviewing before, read one of the many good practical books on interviewing skills. Even better, go on a course for some practice if your training budget will stand it. This list of Dos and Don'ts (Figure 11.1) emphasizes some of the key things to be aware of – or, if you're already a seasoned interviewer, to remember.

Doing a records survey

A records survey is the only way to get hard facts about the volume of records and their physical characteristics. A survey can be very simple, for example, a quick count of how many filing cabinets there are and what type of records they contain. Or it can be very detailed – not only collecting information about the volume of records but about how often they are used and who uses them.

DO

➤ Arrange the interview in a convenient place, ideally away from the interviewee's working environment and in 'neutral territory'.

➤ Set up the interview properly:
  – confirm the date, time and place in writing.
  – state the issues which you will want to cover.
  – inform the interviewee that the interview will be taped, if you have permission to do this.

➤ Do your research and prepare a question plan in advance.

➤ Take enough of everything you might need, such as:
  – writing materials
  – tapes
  – laptop computer
  – background or reference documents
  – business cards
  – personal items (tissues etc.).

➤ Get the comfort factors right if you can:
  – choose the best room or space available
  – arrange the seating appropriately — avoid seats facing windows and in 'confrontational' positions across tables or desks
  – arrange or offer refreshments.

➤ Arrive or be ready on time.

➤ Recap on the purpose of the interview, what you want to cover and how long it will take.

➤ Ask 'open' questions (questions that require more than a one word answer) and vary the style: please explain . . ./tell me . . ./can you clarify . . ./can you comment on . . .

➤ Take care with language. Be particularly careful with humour and sarcasm. Avoid unnecessary jargon and 'buzz-words'.

➤ Listen 'actively' and clarify anything that you don't completely understand.

➤ Distinguish carefully between facts and opinions.

(cont.)

Fig. 11.1 *Interviewing – dos and don'ts*

Interviewing (continued)

- ➤ Keep your own opinions to yourself.
- ➤ Watch the time — finish at the arranged time and arrange another meeting if necessary.
- ➤ 'Leave the door open' to follow-up if you need to.
- ➤ Explain what will happen next.
- ➤ Thank the interviewee for their time and assistance.
- ➤ Write up your notes of the interview as soon as possible afterwards.

DON'T
- ➤ Rush the interview.
- ➤ Allow the interview to wander off on irrelevant tangents.
- ➤ Add issues to the interview 'on the hoof'. If something comes up which you hadn't anticipated, make an appointment for a follow-up session.
- ➤ Waste time — yours or theirs. If it becomes obvious that you're not going to get the information you need, for whatever reason, end the interview politely but positively.
- ➤ Get involved in arguments or debates.
- ➤ Concentrate on taking notes — listen.

The best way to do a survey is to go into departments, talk to staff and look at the records with them. This direct 'face-to-face' approach means that you can ask for all the information you need in one go, and immediately clarify anything that you don't understand. It also gives you the opportunity to sell the benefits of records management and build support for what you need or want to do. However, it is labour-intensive and time-consuming, so if you have to develop policies and systems quickly, it may not be practical. The alternative is to distribute questionnaires for departmental staff to fill in. This indirect approach has obvious disadvantages. People may not respond, or at least not as quickly as you would like them to. They may not answer every question, or take the trouble to get accurate information. If you do decide to send out questionnaires, make them hard to avoid and easy to complete. If possible, make them available electronically, by e-mail or on an intranet, because this generally elicits a better response than paper copies. Even so, you will need patience and persistence to chase for responses and to follow up errors, blanks and things that don't make sense. However you go about it, the keys to success with any records survey are:

1 Visible management support: these days, everyone suffers from 'survey overload'. Getting visible support from management, in the form of memos and team briefings, will raise the profile of what you're doing. And it will give you something to refer to when people say, 'What's all this about, then?'.

2 Well-designed data collection tools: standard forms make collecting and analysing data easier for everyone, provided that they are designed for the job in hand. Figure 11.2 is an example of a records survey form which was used by a team to collect the data required to develop a records retention schedule.

If you have more than one person doing a physical survey, you need to train them to make sure that they all do the same thing in the same way. If you are designing questionnaires for departmental staff to fill in, you should take extra care with the layout and language (avoiding jargon!) and provide very clear instructions on 'how to do it'. Figure 11.3 provides a checklist of some things to remember.

First, decide what you need to know, given the goals which have been set, then decide on the best way to find out, and do it.

RECORDS SURVEY	
Division	
Department	
Title	
Description	
Medium / Format	**Arrangement**
Activity / Use	**Operational Retention Requirements**

Fig. 11.2 *Records survey form*

Questions

Questions should be:

➢ simple
➢ direct
➢ reasonable
➢ expressed in clear unambiguous language
➢ relevant to respondents
➢ arranged in a logical order
➢ numbered.

Questions shouldn't be:
➢ leading
➢ loaded
➢ inappropriate
➢ illegal
➢ impossible to answer.

Instructions
➢ Provide clear instructions for each question. For example,
   – tick one only
   – tick as many as apply
   – describe
   – list
   – comment on.
➢ Provide clear directions on the question path. For example:
   – if No, go to Page 6
   – if Yes, go to Question 4
   – if No, sign the questionnaire and return it to us.
➢ Provide clear instructions for the return of the completed questionnaire. For example:

(cont.)

Fig. 11.3 *Questionnaire design*

Questionnaire design (continued)

    — Return the completed questionnaire in the envelope provided.
    — Send the completed questionnaire to . . .
    — Fax the completed questionnaire to . . . on . . .
    — Send the completed questionnaire to . . . at . . .
➤ Resist the temptation to say 'please' for every question.

Presentation and layout
➤ Resist the temptation to cram the questionnaire into a predetermined number of pages.
➤ Choose a clear, simple font.
➤ Leave wide margins and plenty of white space between questions.
➤ Provide adequate space for unstructured answers. Too little space can irritate — too much can intimidate.

Summary

➤ You need to understand the organization and its business, as well as its records.
➤ There are three basic ways to get the information you need: desk research, interviewing staff and conducting a records survey.

Chapter 12
Now what?

In this chapter you'll find out:

➤ how to identify problems and establish priorities for records management.

Deciding what to do

So you've defined the goals for records management. You've established what your organization does, and how. You know what records it generates and how these are currently managed. Now you can see the gap between the current position and the goals, and work out what to do next.

The gap, and what you should do about it, may seem glaringly obvious to you, but always be suspicious of the 'glaringly obvious' – the bright light at the end of the tunnel is often a train!

There is nothing more deceptive than an obvious fact.

Sir Arthur Conan Doyle

No matter how careful and thorough you were when you were interviewing people and surveying records, it's possible that you might have missed or misunderstood something. It's better to find out sooner rather than later. And finally, remember that you can't be solely responsible for deciding what to do, so you need to be able to demonstrate to management the gap between the current position and the goals, as a basis for collective decision-making. So what you need to do now is some structured analysis.

One of the most useful structured analysis techniques is SWOT analysis. SWOT is an acronym for strengths, weaknesses, opportunities and

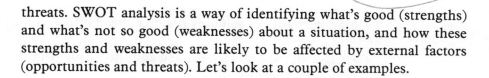

threats. SWOT analysis is a way of identifying what's good (strengths) and what's not so good (weaknesses) about a situation, and how these strengths and weaknesses are likely to be affected by external factors (opportunities and threats). Let's look at a couple of examples.

Management consultancy practice, head office

Goal: Improve the management of project files so that files are always up to date and can be located and retrieved by consultants within five minutes.

SWOT analysis for current filing

Strengths:

➤ Central hard copy files are located within ten metres of the consultants' workstations.
➤ The classification scheme for the central hard copy files is well structured.
➤ Although lots of documents are copied to others within the team and in other teams, there are rules about who is responsible for filing the official copy.

Weaknesses:

➤ The central hard copy files are overloaded with duplicates and junk – stuff that shouldn't be filed at all. It gets filed because nobody can be bothered to think about it.
➤ Documents to be filed in the central hard copy files are put in the secretaries' filing trays. They do the filing once a week or so, as time permits. Sometimes they don't do it for weeks. So the files are usually not up to date.
➤ Electronic filing is 'personal' and everyone admits to not having a clue how to do it properly.
➤ More and more documents are being created by the consultants on laptop computers, because they are spending more and more time out of the office.

(cont.)

Management consultancy practice, head office (continued)

➤ E-mail messages are printed and filed, usually in the central files and in 'personal' files.
➤ Central files are never closed or transferred to storage ('You can never find them again'), and never weeded. It's time-consuming to weed files and there's no retention policy. So some files are very large, some are very old and many are falling to bits.

Opportunities:
➤ The practice is planning to upgrade the IT system and network. This will allow all staff to share electronic files on a single drive.

Threats:
➤ Consultants are spending more time out of the office. Paper documents sit in their in-trays until they come back.
➤ Several consultants are starting to keep personal files on projects and to file documents in these rather than in the official files, so documents are getting lost.
➤ The Administration Manager is looking at electronic document management systems – his plan is to tell everybody to have a clear-out, and then get temps in to scan all the central hard copy files.

Charity, headquarters

Goal: Reduce the volume of current filing by 30%.

SWOT analysis for current filing

Strengths:
➤ When the filing cabinets are full, 'old stuff' is packed into boxes and put into one of the store rooms which are dotted around the office.

(cont.)

Charity, headquarters (continued)

Weaknesses:
➤ There's no standard filing system.
➤ Everybody keeps their own hard copy files, so there's lots of duplication.
➤ Electronic filing is 'personal' – everyone keeps 'their' documents on the C: drive of 'their' PCs.
➤ Nobody ever throws anything away or deletes any electronic documents.
➤ Files are stored in four-drawer filing cabinets next to desks. The top and bottom drawers are usually empty.

Opportunities:
➤ The organization is planning to upgrade the IT system and network. This will enable all staff to share electronic files on a single drive.
➤ The budget for the refurbishment of the office includes money for new filing equipment.

Threats:
➤ One or two managers are very keen on the IT manager's proposal to scan everything, 'then we won't have to worry – we can keep everything forever'.

The results of your SWOT analysis will help you to see *what* needs to be done to correct the weaknesses, to eliminate or reduce the threats and to make the best of the opportunities. The next step is to decide *how* to do it by identifying and evaluating potential solutions. Focus first on what *could* be done. Let's look at our examples again.

Management consultancy practice, head office

Goal: Improve the management of project files so that files are always up to date and can be located and retrieved by consultants within five minutes.

Options:
➢ Develop a records retention policy.
➢ Employ a filing clerk to maintain the central filing systems.
➢ Ban 'personal' files other than informal working papers.
➢ Set up a central electronic filing system, using the same file classification scheme as for the hard copy files, and train all staff to use it.
➢ Provide consultants with dial-in access to the electronic filing system so that they can transfer documents from their laptop computers to shared files on the network quickly and easily.

Charity, headquarters

Goal: Reduce the volume of current filing by 30%.

Options:
➢ Develop a retention policy.
➢ Develop a standard file classification scheme, to be used for both hard copy and electronic records, and train all staff to use it.
➢ Provide clear guidelines on what should NOT be filed.
➢ Set up central hard copy files.
➢ For hard copy files, provide clear guidelines on who should file the official copy of a document (eg the originator of a memo and the principal recipient(s), but not the 'C.C.' recipients.

Then consider what *can* be done. Look at what's possible, and what the constraints may be. For example:

> ➤ there may be no money to employ a filing clerk
> ➤ there may be no obvious space in which to centralize hard copy files, even in higher-density filing cabinets
> ➤ there may be no other storage company in the area which could provide better storage facilities, so you can have good facilities or fast retrieval, but not both.

Now is the time to discuss the options, and your assessment of them, with management. They must make the final decisions, because they have the power to make it happen and the authority to commit the organization to any consequences of their decisions. When the way forward has been agreed, you need to draw up an implementation plan which sets out:

> ➤ tasks – what needs to be done
> ➤ dependencies – how the tasks interrelate (ie before you can do 'b', you need to do 'a')
> ➤ timescale – how long it will take
> ➤ resources – what resources will be needed, eg money (how much? when?), time (whose? how much? when?).

If you don't have much experience of planning or managing projects, read Liz MacLachlan's excellent *Making project management work for you* in this series (Library Association Publishing, 1996) before you go any further.

Summary

> ➤ Always be suspicious of the 'glaringly obvious'.
> ➤ Remember that you can't be solely responsible for deciding what to do.
> ➤ Identify and evaluate all the options – don't rule anything out too soon.
> ➤ Records management, like so many things, is the art of the possible.

Chapter 13
First things first!
Developing the framework of policies and procedures

In this chapter you'll find out:

➤ **how to develop records management policies and procedures.**

If your organization has never 'done' records management before, you'll need to establish a framework of policies and procedures to ensure that whatever is done initially becomes 'the way we do things around here' and not just 'something we tried once'. Once the framework is in place, you need to make sure that everybody understands what they have to do and how to do it by providing appropriate training for them. Again, there's nothing new here if you've been involved in managing or operating a library or information service, so just a quick recap on the main points.

Policies

A records management policy sets out

1 the purpose of the policy
   – why the organization needs a policy
2 the scope of the policy
   – the parts of the organization, the sites and the types of records covered by the policy
3 responsibilities for developing and implementing the policy
   – the specific responsibilities of senior executives (ultimately responsible and accountable for the organization's actions), line management (directly responsible for implementing the policy

within their areas of responsibility), staff with specific records management responsibilities (for example, filing), and others

4 the procedures for implementing the policy
- the procedures to be followed, and where they can be found
- how those responsible for the implementation of the policy will check that it's being applied, and what actions they will take if they find that it isn't
- how often the policy, or any part of it, will be reviewed.

Policies don't need to be long or complex. In fact, the shorter and simpler they are, the better, because they're more likely to be read!

Procedures

Procedures must be simple and set out in a straightforward way, indicating both what is to be done and who is to do it. As a rule, it's better to have more simple steps than fewer complicated ones. Figure 13.1 is a good example.

Once you've developed policies and procedures, think about training.

Training

The most effective way to train anybody to do anything is to:

➢ tell them what to do
➢ show them how to do it
➢ let them do it, with clear written instructions to refer back to
➢ check how they're getting on and correct if necessary.

Think about it. It's always easier to cook a Delia Smith recipe from the book when you've seen her do it on TV. Actually, Delia's most recent series *How to Cook* is a good analogy for training in 'how to use the records management system'. The series was much derided in the press as 'How to Boil Water', and you may find that your offers of 'training' are also pooh-poohed. Yes, we're back to that old 'records management = filing' thing again, and everyone knows how to file, don't they? The

Step 1	Decide what records are to be sent to the store.	User
Step 2	Phone the records coordinator to ask for a records storage box to be delivered.	User
Step 3	Check that the user understands the procedure for transferring records to off-site storage, and that s/he knows how to assemble and pack a records storage box. Arrange delivery of a records storage box to the user.	Records coordinator
Step 4	Assemble the records storage box and pack the records into it.	User
Step 5	List the contents of the records storage box on a records transmittal list.	User
Step 6	Phone the records coordinator to request collection of the box.	User
Step 7	Arrange collection of the box from the user.	Records coordinator
Step 8	Check that the records transmittal list is completed correctly. If it is incorrect or incomplete return the box to the user.	Records coordinator
Step 9	Enter the data from the records transmittal list onto the records management database.	Records coordinator
Step 10	Add the details of the records storage box to the collection docket for the storage company.	Records coordinator
Step 11	Release the box to the storage company driver, obtaining his/her signature.	Records coordinator
Step 12	File the collection docket.	Records coordinator

Fig. 13.1 *Transferring records to off-site storage*

fact is, most records management procedures just aren't complicated enough! So think creatively – there may be several ways to get your message across. Getting the tone right is important. Instead of 'training sessions', how about 'briefing sessions' or 'workshops'? How about offering incentives to turn up? Food and drink usually work quite well – try 'breakfast briefings' or something similar. Remember that people will sign up for half an hour more readily than a whole hour, so keep sessions short. Above all, don't give anyone an excuse not to come by choosing the wrong day or time of day. Ask people when they want to come and either choose the most popular time or offer alternatives. Do what you can to persuade people to take the 'training' on offer, and don't resort to the management three-line-whip unless you absolutely have to.

Summary

➤ Think of records management as a tent – put the frame together properly before you start wrestling with the canvas.

➤ Keep policies and procedures short and simple – they're more likely to be read that way.

➤ Offer everyone the opportunity to learn what to do and how to do it .

➤ Think creatively about how to get the messages across.

Chapter 14
Everyone's a customer
Providing records management services

> **In this chapter you'll find out:**
>
> ➤ **how you can support the implementation of records management policies and procedures**
> ➤ **the critical success factors for records management services.**

To support the implementation of your organization's records management policies and procedures, you'll need to:

> ➤ raise the profile of records and records management – and keep it up!
> ➤ provide advice on all aspects of records management and other records-related issues
> ➤ provide support services to deal with routine tasks efficiently and effectively.

Raising the profile

Even with the best will in the world, organizing records is rarely at the top of people's 'To Do' lists. Even when they know how important records are, and what they have to do with them, most people still need a nudge to actually do it. The key word is 'encouragement' – you need to keep records management in everyone's sights and remind them regularly to do what they need to do. The tone needs to be lightweight, giving information as much as direction. Things which work well include:

> eye-catching leaflets on key topics
> key messages printed on things staff actually use, such as mugs, mouse mats and desk diaries
> topical briefing or training sessions for staff, either as 'one-off' events or incorporated into routine internal communications programmes
> short articles on key topics in in-house magazines
> well-structured pages on intranets.

Be careful with humour – it can work well or it can be a disaster. Above all, resist the temptation to be frivolous – it only adds to that widespread view that 'records management = filing'.

Providing advice

When it comes to providing advice, you must be proactive as well as reactive. From time to time, managers will need advice on:

> designing and managing filing systems
> storing current and inactive records
> retaining records to meet operational, legal and regulatory requirements
> identifying and protecting vital records
> destroying records which are no longer needed
> converting records to another medium to improve efficiency or effectiveness or to save space or money
> recruiting and training staff to do records work

as a basis for strategic planning, to resolve operational problems or to support specific projects such as an office relocation, a major legal case or the introduction of new information technology. The question is, 'When they realize that they need advice, will they know that you can provide it, or direct them to someone who can?' To make sure that they will know, you must take every opportunity that comes your way to make them aware of what records management is about, and what you can do.

So do the '90s thing – network! Establish good relationships with managers in areas such as facilities, purchasing, legal compliance and IT. The more people who know what you can do and the help you can give, the more opportunities you'll get to do it. Scan the newspapers and current affairs journals for records-related features and news – things like new technologies, changes in legislation or how other similar organizations are managing their records. You can pass these on to appropriate people with a 'Have you seen this?' or 'I thought you might be interested in this because . . .' note. You can also use them as a basis for short pieces in in-house magazines, newsy items on the intranet and so on. This will keep records management in the sights of management and raise your profile as someone who can advise on these issues. So you need to make sure that you keep up to date with developments in the records management field by reading the journals, going to meetings and training events, joining Internet discussion lists, etc. Above all, be brutally honest about the limits of your knowledge and expertise and, if you can't deal with a particular issue, consult a professional records manager.

Providing services

Managing records efficiently and effectively takes commitment, time and effort. Depending on how they were managed before, the introduction of good records management policies and procedures may actually make some routine tasks more, rather than less, complex and time-consuming for staff at the 'front end'. For example:

> ➢ instead of just filing electronic documents any old way on the C: drive of a PC, they have to file them in a shared directory on the computer network, using standard file-naming conventions;
> ➢ instead of just filing documents in their personal files, they have to file documents in the central files and only keep copies for themselves. Worse, the central files are on a different floor, so filing and retrieving records takes ages;

➤ instead of just dropping records into a box and getting George to take it down to the basement, the records have to be listed on a form, the box has to be packed in a particular way, etc etc.

Of course we know that this additional effort 'up front' will save time and trouble later. However, the people who actually have to do these things every day don't always see the big picture, particularly if it's not obvious what's in it for them.

A critical success factor for records management is making it easy for people to do what needs to be done. One way is to use dedicated, trained staff to provide services which take many of the routine tasks off people's hands. This is a 'win-win' approach. First, the essential tasks get done promptly and properly, and often more efficiently and economically because of the economies of scale. For instance, if the central files are at the other end of the building, it makes sense to wait until you've got several things to file before you go to do it. If inactive records are stored off-site with a storage company, it makes sense to wait for several requests for items before you ring up, to avoid paying for five journeys when one will do. Second, the time which would be spent on these routine tasks by other staff can be better used to improve their, and the organization's, productivity.

The range of services

The most common records management services are:

1 Managing active filing systems, involving:
   – opening files
   – closing files
   – collecting documents for filing
   – classifying documents, or advising staff on classification
   – filing
   – retrieving documents and files on request
   – destroying redundant documents and files.
2 Managing storage facilities for inactive records, and providing retrieval services, involving:

- packing and listing hard copy records to go into storage, or advising users on the procedure
- transferring inactive electronic records to offline media if necessary, or advising those responsible for the computer systems when this is required
- transferring records to storage
- retrieving records from storage on request
- collecting records when users have finished with them, and returning them to storage.

3 Managing the destruction of records, involving:
- collecting records for destruction
- authorizing destruction, or obtaining approval from appropriate management
- destroying records, or organizing collection by a third-party destruction contractor
- overseeing destruction if required.

Other services you could offer include managing the conversion of records to alternative media, for example, by scanning or microfilming.

Providing a records management service is essentially the same as providing any other kind of service. You need to:

➢ identify your customers and establish their needs
➢ decide what service, and what level of service, to provide and how to deliver it
➢ market the service
➢ deliver the service
➢ monitor and evaluate the service to ensure that it continues to meet customers' needs.

There are plenty of good books about planning, marketing and delivering services, so look at some of these if you don't have much experience in this area. Here are a just a few specific issues to think about in relation to records management services.

Customers

The 'point of delivery' customers for records management services are the staff, but the real customer for records management is 'the organization'. Its needs come first and determine what has to be done, whether individual members of staff like it or not. If they don't like it, they will still have to use your service, even though they haven't asked for it, don't like it and don't want it. You'll need all your interpersonal skills to deal with this challenge. In particular, give a lot of thought to . . .

Marketing

Remember that your customers don't have a choice about whether to use your service or not. So your marketing strategy needs to focus on the fact that the service you are providing makes it as easy and painless as possible for them to do what they have to do. Present the benefits in their terms, like this, for example:

> ➢ 'You'll have more time to do your "real" work.'
> ➢ 'You won't have to waste time going up and down the stairs/phoning down to the basement.'
> ➢ 'You'll always know exactly where your files are.'
> ➢ 'You won't have to worry about filing any more – we'll do it all for you.'
> ➢ 'You'll be able to get your files whenever you want them.'

As far as marketing records management services to the managers who have to pay for them is concerned, focus on the big cost-benefit picture. Having a team of dedicated staff to do some of the routine tasks involved in managing records means that other staff can concentrate on their core work, and will therefore be more productive. This is a particular benefit for highly qualified professional and technical staff. For instance, filing even electronic documents is probably not the best use of a senior engineer's time. A filing clerk costs a lot less to employ than a senior engineer. The additional cost of employing one filing clerk to do filing for 20 engineers may be justified by the benefits – more productive use of 20 engineers' time, improved control of their records (since they probably

163

wouldn't have done the filing anyway!), and faster and more certain access to the information contained in them.

Once your marketing strategy is sorted out, all you have to do is make sure that you deliver what you promise and keep in touch with your customers' needs over time. In fact, most organizations find that once records management services become established, they become indispensable.

Management

When you're planning records management services, focus first on *what* needs to be provided, then on *who* should be responsible for providing it and managing it. It may make sense to establish a records management department, in which case you'll need to decide where this would best fit within the organizational structure. The original impetus for records management may have come from, say, the information centre, but the information manager may not be the most appropriate person to take on responsibility for providing records management services. If setting up a records management department is not a realistic option, you'll need to decide which department should take responsibility for providing records management services. The most logical solution may be for different departments to take responsibility for different services. Basically, if the service is the right service, and if it meets the objectives of making sure that records are managed efficiently, effectively and economically, it doesn't matter who manages it, *provided that* the manager concerned is committed to it and prepared to give it the attention and resources it deserves. Too often, records management services revert to being 'just filing' or 'just archiving' – not sexy, not interesting, not worthy of time or attention until there's a crisis. This is no way to treat the organization's most important information resource. Whoever is responsible for providing records management services must realize how important they are.

Staff

When you've decided what services to provide and what service levels to offer, you'll need to think about staffing. Just as you would with any other role, start by defining it. What is the job? What knowledge, qualifications, skills, experience and personal attributes are required to do it? Depending on the service you're providing, you might need a graduate with a professional qualification in records management, three years' experience, good IT skills and a driving licence or someone with good GCSEs, 40 wpm typing, experience of using computer databases and a good telephone manner. Then it's time to present your case to management for approval of recruitment or redeployment of existing staff. This is often where the trouble starts: you may have trouble convincing management that you haven't over-specified the requirements for the job, especially if you are requesting someone with professional qualifications. You may find yourself under pressure to take on people from other parts of the organization who are clearly not suitable but who are currently under-utilized or about to be made redundant. However, stick to your guns. Presumably the organization doesn't normally recruit people who don't meet job specifications, so why should this job be any different? You need someone who's interested and committed to handling the organization's most important information resource. There really are people out there who enjoy doing records work, and are good at it. You just have to find them.

Internal relationships

Depending on what records management services you provide, you may be dependent on the cooperation and support of other internal service providers. For example:

> ➤ If you provide a filing service which involves collecting hard copy documents for filing, you may want the actual collection to be done by the internal mail messengers as part of their mail round.
> ➤ If you provide a service which involves managing electronic documents, you will need to work with the IT department who control and maintain hardware and software.
> ➤ If you manage an off-site storage facility for inactive records, you may need to use pool vehicles to get to and from the site.

> If you are responsible for managing a contract with a commercial storage company, you may need to work with the purchasing department to set up the contract, and possibly with your internal auditors to check that the contractor is performing as required.
> If you want to provide retrieval and delivery services, you may need to work with your internal mail and messenger services.
> If you organize destruction of records, you may need to liaise with the departments responsible for housekeeping and waste disposal.

Building good working relationships with the people you depend on to be able to provide a quality service yourself, is a solid investment.

Like all services, when records management services are working well, they should blend into the background to become just part of 'the way we do things around here'. And like all services, getting them to work this smoothly takes a lot of time and effort.

Summary

> Raising awareness of records management is vital, so be proactive – look for opportunities to promote good practice – and draw attention to bad practice!
> Providing services is providing services is providing services, but remember that some of your 'customers' might rather not be your customers (nothing personal, of course).
> Like all services, when records management services are working well, people should barely notice them.

Appendix 1
Getting help – a list of useful addresses

Managing records involves making or facilitating decisions about lots of things. If you're not a professional records manager, you'll need help from a variety of sources.

Professional organizations

In the UK, the **Society of Archivists** is the professional organization for archivists and records managers. It has a number of special interest groups which you can contact for help and advice. The Society's central office may be able to put you in touch with individual members in similar organizations. The Society also maintains a list of members who offer consultancy services.

Alternatively, anyone working in the records management field can belong to The **Records Management Society**. Its members include professional archivists and records managers, consultants and suppliers of records management services and products. Its membership list is categorized by location and sector, and is a useful way of finding contacts in organizations similar to your own.

Both the Society of Archivists and the Records Management Society have useful publications and organize training events which non-members may attend. Contact details for them can be found in the following list of organizations.

Suppliers of goods and services

Suppliers of goods and services can be a source of information. Companies selling all kinds of things now offer the services of their 'consultants' to help you to 'decide what you need'. However, a 'consultant' who is paid by a potential supplier may only be a sales representative with a better suit. Beware and ask yourself:

➢ are they starting with my needs and working forwards, or their product and working backwards?
➢ if I buy this, what do they get?

Consultants

Consultants who are *professionally-qualified* and *genuinely independent* will be able to give you high-quality, impartial, tailored advice on records management. The key words are in *italics*, so check these characteristics and make sure that they have experience which is relevant to your requirements. Both the Society of Archivists and the Records Management Society can help you to find a consultant.

Contact details

Society of Archivists Records Management Group
Contact: Executive Secretary
Address: 40 Northampton Road
              London ECIR 0HB
              UK
Tel: +44 (0)20 7278 8630
Fax: +44 (0)20 7278 2107
E-mail: *societyofarchivists@archives.org.uk*
URL: *http://www.societyofarchivists.org.uk*

Records Management Society of Great Britain (RMS)
Contact: Administration Secretary
Address: Woodside
              Coleheath Bottom
              Speen
              Princes Risborough HP27 0SZ
              UK
Tel: +44 1494 488599
Fax: +44 1494 488590

E-mail: *rms@awdry.demon.co.uk*
URL: *http://www.rms-gb.org.uk*

Business Archives Council (BAC)
Address: 101 Whitechapel High Street
            London E1 7RE
            UK
Tel: +44 (0)20 7247 0024
Fax: +44 (0)20 7422 0026
E-mail: *bac@archives.gla.ac.uk*
URL: *http://www.archives.gla.ac.uk/bac/*

International Records Management Council (IRMC)
Address: Church Bank
            Main Street
            Holcot
            Northampton NN6 9SP
            UK
Tel: +44 1604 781250
Fax: +44 1604 781973
E-mail: *charman.irm@btinternet.com*

Association of Records Managers and Administrators (ARMA), Inc.
Address: 4200 Somerset Drive
            Suite 215
             Prairie Village
            KS 66208
            USA
Tel: +1 913 341 3808
Fax: +1 913 341 3742
E-mail: *hq@arma.org*
URL: *http://www.arma.org./*

International Records Management Trust

Address:	12 John Street
	London WC1N 2EB
	UK
Tel:	+44 (0)20 7831 4101
Fax:	+44 (0)20 7831 7404
E-mail:	*irmt@sas.ac.uk*
URL:	*http://www.irmt.org/*

Records Management Association of Australia

Address:	Reply Paid No. 1
	Records Management Association of Australia
	PO Box 97
	Bondall Heights Qld 4034
	Australia
Tel:	+61 7 3965 1611
Fax:	+61 7 3965 1611
E-mail:	*rmaasec@rmaa.com.au*
URL:	*http://www.rmaa.com.au*

Aslib (The Association for Information Management)

Address:	Staple Hall
	Stone House Court
	London EC3A 7PB
	UK
Tel:	+44 (0)20 7903 0000
Fax:	+44 (0)20 7903 0011
E-mail:	*aslib@aslib.co.uk*
URL:	*http://www.aslib.co.uk*

Appendix 2
Case study: the importance of records management

T&N plc

J W Roberts Ltd was established as a family firm in 1870. Their factory in Armley, Leeds produced asbestos lagging for steam engines. In 1920 the company merged with Turner & Newall Ltd, then the world's largest manufacturer of asbestos products. Turner & Newall subsequently diversified into automotive engineering, becoming T&N plc.

In 1994 June Hancock discovered that she was suffering from mesothelioma, a rare form of lung cancer for which the only known cause is exposure to asbestos. As a child, she had lived and played beside the Roberts' Armley factory between 1938 and 1951. She brought a suit against J W Roberts Ltd claiming damages for personal injury caused by exposure to asbestos from the factory. A similar claim was brought by Evelyn Margereson, suing for the loss of her husband who had died of mesothelioma in 1991, claiming that he too had been exposed to asbestos from the factory as a child.

The lawyers for Hancock and Margereson needed to prove that T&N, and its subsidiary J W Roberts, knew of the risks from exposure to asbestos dust in the 1940s and 1950s. This became an uphill task as T&N vigorously fought attempts to reveal internal company documents in the discovery process. They initially said that they were having problems in identifying key records among the 27,000 or so documents which were potentially relevant to the case. They then said that there were no relevant documents. The case was effectively stalled and could not have been pursued had it not been for a related case in the US. Chase Manhattan Bank launched an action against T&N for $185m in damages relating to the use of asbestos in their New York headquarters building in 1959. US legal discovery processes enabled Chase to demand documents from T&N's Manchester headquarters as part of their legal action, and they made these documents available to the lawyers for Hancock and Margereson.

More than 50,000 documents were handed over, ranging from internal memoranda to minutes of meetings. These documents provided damning evidence that the company had deliberately prevaricated about the dangers of asbestos and had tried to resist new government safety regulations. In 1931 the government introduced new safety regulations for asbestos plants after it was found that more than a quarter of asbestos workers had lung damage. These regulations required the use of extractor fans in all plants wherever a worker was exposed to asbestos dust on more than an occasional basis, defined as once a week. That same year, Samuel Turner wrote to Frederick Newall 'I feel this definition of occasional is rather too strict. We must take a small risk by stretching the regulations for our own ends.' Records showed that T&N were aware of the risks of asbestos in the early 1930s, and knew in 1943 that asbestos was a danger to the public, not just to workers. A T&N internal memo from 1974 said, 'We hope very much we will never be called upon to discuss Armley in the public arena.'

In October 1995 the High Court ordered T&N to pay £115,000 damages to Hancock and Margereson. Mr Justice Holland ruled that from 1933 onwards the defendants must have known of the dangers of asbestos dust and had taken no reasonable steps to reduce or prevent emissions from their factory in Armley. His judgment was that the company owed a duty of care to all those living in the immediate vicinity of the Armley factory, and would be liable to pay damages to future victims of mesothelioma who had lived close to the factory, given that the incubation period for the disease is up to 60 years.

This case was hailed as a landmark which opened the way for up to 40 others who had developed asbestos-related illnesses after exposure to asbestos dust near the factory. T&N paid the damages as awarded 'without prejudice' but appealed against the ruling. The Court of Appeal upheld the Holland judgment in April 1996.

The asbestos issue dogged the company for more than a decade. Its reputation was seriously damaged. In the ten years to 1996, it paid out a total of over £350m in settlement of personal injury claims for asbestos-related illnesses, mostly in the US. Fears of further payouts after the Hancock & Margereson case and unfavourable US court rulings undermined the share price. The company's efforts to reposition itself as an 'asbestos-free' engineering company were consistently frustrated. Some commentators believe that T&N survived the crisis because it was a substantial company which had already diversified its business into a high-margin sector. The financial claims on them had relatively little impact. For a less financially robust organization, receivership may have been inevitable.

RECORDS SERIES	FILE CODE
1. Accident Reports	6.1.2
2. Boiler Inspection Certificates	6.5.3
3. Boiler Maintenance Contracts	6.5.3
4. Car Insurance Claims	2.5.2
5. Car Insurance Policies	2.5.2
6. Insurance Policies	6.2
7. Window Cleaning Schedules	6.6.1
8. Maintenance Schedules	6.5
9. Lift Service Reports	6.5.1
10. Fire Drill Notifications	6.1
11. Induction Course Materials	2.2.1
12. Milk Round Schedules	2.1.6
13. Waste Collection Certificates	6.6.2
14. Safety Audit Reports	6.1.1
15. Staff Photographs	6.3
16. Training Course Bookings	2.2.2
17. Unsuccessful Applications	2.1.1
18. Vehicle Accident Reports	6.2.3
19. Visitors Books	6.3
20. Minutes of the Health & Safety Committee	6.1

Fig. 2.1(c) *Filing system references (a small service company) (see pages 23–5)*

Further reading

Books

There are a number of books on the theory and practice of records management. These are some of the most recent and useful. If you are looking for more detailed information on any of the topics in this book, I suggest you start here.

Kennedy, J and Schauder, C, *Records management*, Addison-Wesley Longman Higher Education, 1998.

Robek, M F, Brown, G F and Stephens, D O, *Information and records management: document-based information systems*, 4th edn, Glencoe McGraw-Hill, 1995.

Appendix E contains an extensive list of records management publications.

Diamond, S Z, *Records management: a practical guide*, AMACOM, 1995.

Penn, I, Pennix, G and Coulson, J, *Records management handbook*, Gower Press, 1994.

Sampson, K L, *Value-added records management*, Quorum Books, 1992

Emmerson, P (ed), *How to manage your records: a guide to effective practice*, ICSA Publishing, 1989

Journals

These are the key journals in the field.

Bulletin: Records Management Society

Records management journal: ASLIB

Records management quarterly: Association of Records Managers and Administrators, Inc.

InfoRMAA: Records Management Association of Australia

Information management & technology: CIMTECH Ltd.

Standards

There are hundreds of national and international standards which are potentially relevant to records management activities. Depending on where you are, and the issue in question, you will need to check with the relevant national standards bodies. This is a list of some of the most important standards which you should be familiar with if you are working in the UK.

BS 5454:1989 Recommendations for storage and exhibition of archival documents

BS 6498:1991 Guide to preparation of microfilm and other microforms that may be required as evidence

BS 4783:Parts 1-8 Storage, transportation and maintenance of media for use in data processing and information storage

BS 7768:1994 Recommendations for management of optical disk (WORM) systems for the recording of documents that may be required as evidence

DISC PD 0008:1999 Code of practice for legal admissibility of information stored electronically

DISC PD 0010:1997 The guide to good practice in information management

You should also be aware of the Australian Records Management Standard AS 4390.1 – 1996. Work is in progress to make this the basis of an international standard.

Websites

The Association of Records Managers and Administrators (ARMA) Rio Grande Chapter maintains the superb Records and Information Management Resource List, which contains links to thousands of records and information management and other related websites **http://www.flash.net/~survivor/sitefram.htm.**

Videos

Buried Alive: Document Retention

Commonwealth Films Inc.
223 Commonwealth Avenue
Boston
Massachusetts 02116
USA

Records Management Service

University of Liverpool
Liverpool L69 3BX
United Kingdom

Records Management Concepts
Electronic Recordkeeping
Records Retention & Disposition Schedule

Edith Cowan University
Pearson Street
Churchlands 6018
Western Australia

Index